NEW AGE CAPITALISM

NEW AGE CAPITALISM

Making Money East of Eden

Kimberly J. Lau

PENN

University of Pennsylvania Press

Philadelphia

Printed in the United States of America on acid-free paper

10 9 8 7 6 5 4 3 2 1

Published by
University of Pennsylvania Press
Philadelphia, Pennsylvania 19104-4011

Library of Congress Cataloging-in-Publication Data

Lau, Kimberly J.
New age capitalism : making money east of Eden / Kimberly J. Lau.
p. cm.
Includes bibliographical references and index.
ISBN 0-8122-3548-7 (alk. paper). — ISBN 0-8122-1729-2 (pbk.: alk. paper)
1. New age consumers—United States. 2. Capitalism—Social aspects—United States. 3. Consumption (Economics)—Social aspects—United States. 4. Marketing—United States. I. Title.

HC110.C6 L38 2000 99-058206
658.8'00973—dc21 CIP

For

James Lau

(1938–1995)

Hero, Father, Friend

Contents

1

IDEOLOGY INCORPORATED

From Bodily Practice to Body Product

In 1946, an alcoholic, drug-addicted veteran of World War II happened to meet a world-famous yogi in a Los Angeles hotel.[1] The chance meeting had a transformative effect on the shell-shocked veteran, who returned to his native South Africa taken with the idea of yoga. After years of studying hatha yoga and kriya breathing techniques through home courses and later with a yogi in India, the veteran, Mani Finger, became a swami and a yogi and developed the Ishta (Integral Science of Hatha and Tantric Arts) system of yoga which is recognized internationally today.

Soon after Mani Finger became a yogi, an obese fifteen-year-old boy turned to him for yoga instruction in an attempt to remedy his many health problems—psychosomatic conditions that Western biomedicine and psychiatry had failed to relieve. The boy was Alan Finger, his son. Yoga cured Alan of his ailments, and father and son practiced and taught together for the next fifteen years until Alan moved to Los Angeles in the mid-1970s.

Alan Finger began teaching yoga to Hollywood stars and in 1987 co-founded Yoga Works, a large studio in Santa Monica. Today, Yoga Works operates two studios in Santa Monica, and together they offer 152 classes each week. Classes are $14, except for a few "community classes" offered during slower parts of the day for $5. At these rates, with the current number of students, large yoga centers like Yoga Works can gross around $30,000 a week. Alan Finger is no longer involved with Yoga Works, but that doesn't mean he's not capitalizing on the popularity he partially helped to create. After leaving California for New York, Finger opened a new studio called Yoga Zone. Yoga Zone is now the world's only yoga studio franchise, with branches in

New York and California and locations planned for Chicago and other major cities. Yoga Zone also has a mail-order catalogue that offers the company's own line of yoga clothing—prominently featuring the Yoga Zone logo—as well as yoga props, instructional videos, books, CDs, and miscellaneous yoga-inspired New Age kitsch. In 1997, the annual sales for Yoga Zone were close to $3 million.[2]

The story of Mani and Alan Finger is, in many ways, also the story of what has happened to yoga in the United States in the past thirty years. Yoga's social status has changed with its movement from the cultural periphery, where it was most commonly perceived as a countercultural practice for hippies, flower children, and "granolas," to its place in the cultural center with its links to hip movie stars and musicians and upscale urban studios; even Fortune 500 companies are inviting yoga instructors to teach classes on site for their employees. While most yoga centers and instructional videos downplay yoga's explicit origins in Hindu sacred texts in an attempt to distance themselves from the yoga of the 1970s, they still pitch their advertising to the seemingly insatiable market for things "eastern" which has emerged with a special force in the 1990s. In fact, this is the epitome of New Age capitalism.

This book investigates the tension that exists between the self-proclaimed spirituality of "alternative" health practices like yoga and the ways in which such practices have been transformed into commodities for a market economy. Yoga is, of course, just one example, and I discuss it, together with t'ai chi, in more detail below (see Chapter 4). The two other cases of New Age Capitalism that I consider are aromatherapy and macrobiotic eating (see Chapters 2 and 3). Together, the three cases suggest some reasons for the popularity of New Age capitalism in the 1990s and lay bare some of the ideologies at work in the media forms that sustain the vitality of these practices. In the final chapter, I discuss the serious cultural and political consequences of New Age capitalism for a democratic society.

Bodies Personal and Politic: Alternative Health and Promises of Transformation

The pursuit of health and wellness runs deep in the texts and textures of contemporary daily life in the United States. First thing in the morning, cereal boxes promise to reduce the risk of heart disease, and orange juice cartons herald the juice's ability to ward off cancer. Aromatherapy soaps and lotions are designed to uplift the spirits in preparation for the stresses of daily toil or to wash them away at the end of the day. Suggestions for healthy living are regular features on television and radio programs and in magazines and newspapers. As a popular and fundamental part of everyday life, the pursuit of health and wellness is dispersed from the specialized realm of medical doctors and Western biomedicine to the broader domain of alternative strategies for holistic living.

In this way, exercise regimens are made of Eastern philosophies through the conversion of holistic practices like yoga and t'ai chi. Belief systems become healthy, low-impact exercises as well as training advantages for professional football and basketball players. Superfoods derived from vaguely identified traditions of herbal medicine and special diets based on ancient and/or remote non-Western cultures suggest themselves as cures for everything from the common cold to cancer, as antidotes for memory loss, stress, and aging. The prevalence and presence of the alternatives cannot be ignored. If you don't practice yoga or t'ai chi, you probably know someone who does. If you haven't had an aromatherapy massage, a friend has probably told you where—and especially why—to get one. Perhaps you follow a strict macrobiotic diet or maybe you have tried one of the macrobiotic options at the Ritz Carlton while on vacation. Regardless, you've probably read about some of these practices and products in a newspaper, magazine, or unsolicited mail-order catalogue. Proclamations of the wise ways of alternative health and holistic living saturate contemporary life in the United States.

Implicit in the popular discourses surrounding aromatherapy, macrobiotic eating, and yoga and t'ai chi is the belief in personal transformation through alternative, non-Western paradigms of health and wellness. Through what Robert Cantwell calls a physical and sensory "ethnomimesis"—that is, the imitation of another culture's traditions and practices—the rhetoric of holistic living is both operationalized and internalized.[3]

The experiential quality of this bodily ethnomimesis allows people to render their own bodies foreign, to "yield into and become Other,"[4] to encourage their bodies to become, very literally, the "other" bodies commonly associated with these practices. In this way, the processes and practices of mimesis create a symbolic world in which the experiences of the miming culture are central and other worlds and other people are absorbed to suit it.[5] Thus, where bodily practices like macrobiotic eating or t'ai chi are concerned, the transformative experience of making the body foreign is refracted through the lens of the familiar, and it is mainly through the practices of "the other" that people transform their bodies so as to achieve the size, shape, and states of physical and emotional health that are culturally valued in the West.

Not only personal health and wellness are to be transformed through the mimetic consumption of foreign bodily practices, however. These practices are also upheld as ways of remedying social and environmental illnesses. Thus, aromatherapy products are celebrated for their eco-friendliness, and certain Aveda brand lipsticks—premised on the principles of aromatherapy—are marketed with the information that the pigments used in their production are harvested in conjunction with the Yawanawa people of the Brazilian rainforest. Similarly, yoga and t'ai chi are presented as means of promoting enhanced social relations by reducing individual stress, and macrobiotic eating is upheld for its insistence on organic foods, an aspect of the diet that contributes not only to the economic survival of small farms but also to the protection of the earth's lands from dangerous pesticides. Through the discursive fields in which these bodily practices are embedded, personal transformations become political as social and planetary wellness is directly correlated with individual health.

At the heart of this drive for bodily—and thus, personal, social, and planetary—transformations are the American traditions of self-reliance and individualism. Together, they create a spirit in which the desire for continual self-transformation can be imagined within broader social contexts, as applicable to the body politic. The discourses of these bodily practices are not the first to promote personal, social, even planetary health through the individual and his or her efforts to refashion the body. In many cases, nineteenth-century American social reformers linked their causes with health reform in a move that made explicit the axiomatic relationship between the individual body and the body politic.[6] For health reformers, in particular, the health of the nation paralleled the health of the individual. This belief was a driving force behind social movements like Muscular Christianity and social phenomena like patent medicines and breakfast cereals as cures for constipation.[7]

In the United States, the Muscular Christianity movement of the late 1800s represented the coalescence of the burgeoning interest in physical fitness and the spirit of religious revivals popular during the second half of the nineteenth century. The logic motivating the movement advocated bodily perfection as "an essential part of Christian morality" and as a means by which "human action could determine individual and social salvation."[8] And yet, the success of the movement owed as much to images of physical weakness—on individual and national levels—as it did to promises of religious salvation. Together with the American traditions of self-reliance and individualism, easily converted into the rhetoric of self-help, the image of physical weakness motivated people to take action. In large part, the Muscular Christianity movement was aimed at middle- and upper-class Northeasterners whose work in offices represented their advanced positions, particularly with respect to "less developed civilizations," but which ultimately rendered them "mentally overtax[ed]" and physically weak.[9] Through the physical fitness regimens at the heart of the Muscular Christianity movement, young professionals could "increase their energy and improve their life and, implicitly, their afterlife."[10] The Muscular Christianity movement epitomizes the belief in individual bodily transformation as crucial to the transformation of the body politic, an imagined social and collective reality made material through popular images of strength and health.[11] Here, media images exemplify the power of mimesis in constructing and maintaining dominant ideologies about American bodies.[12] The socially imagined correlation between the individual body and the body politic was powerful and pervasive enough to inspire the development of physical education programs, the YMCA movement, public gymnasiums, and city playgrounds.[13]

Dietary reform efforts around the turn of the century and into the early 1900s also emphasized the relationship between personal health and social wellness.[14] Health faddists who advocated a wide range of often competing remedies for social malaise found common ground in their criticisms of the American diet, which they believed contributed directly to "the debilitated condition of American men and women."[15] The body was most commonly thematized as a machine, exemplified by the popularity of Henry Ford's Model T and his assembly-line system of factory production, and as a machine, the body required the proper fuels, maintenance, and cleaning to run efficiently. Within the logic of this model, constipation was identified as the predominant cause of illness, loss of energy, and even premature death. Fortunately, "autointoxication" could be avoided in a variety of ways—eating the proper breakfast cereals, following the right diets, fletcherizing (chewing food until all of its flavor is extracted and then involuntarily swallowing it), taking laxatives and other patent medicines, even relying on mechanical solutions like contraptions for "internal bathing." It is precisely these types of dietary fads—the inexpensive diets, the conveniently pre-packaged superfoods, the gimmicks like fletcherizing—which intimately linked the spirit of self-help with interests in personal health. These early fascinations with self-help, food, and health are practically reproduced intact in contemporary discourses of macrobiotic eating, superfoods like bran, and all manner of diets (and especially those outlin-ing specific food combinations). Then—as now—dietary restrictions were powerful means of transforming the body for both personal and social ends.

The extent of personal transformation accomplished through aromatherapy, macrobiotic eating, yoga, and t'ai chi ranges from specific beauty and health remedies to a whole way of life. One might practice yoga with the intention of creating a leaner, stronger body or one might move to a yoga commune where the philosophy behind yoga offers a complete lifestyle; one might eat at a macrobiotic restaurant occasionally or one might follow the strictest macrobiotic diet. It is only at the most radical ends of the continuum that practitioners create seemingly whole alternatives to the familiar structures of everyday life in the United States. And yet, even the more radical interpretations of these bodily practices open themselves up to the processes of commodification. A way of life becomes another commodity to consume and to sell. With New Age capitalism, the instructional products, brochures for niche tourism, and even the more banal logos, t-shirts, caps, and pins associated with these alternative health practices come to mark the contemporary consumer landscape in which our bodies themselves become part of the signage.[16]

Popular Orientalism and Natural Fantasies: Critiquing Modernity

Though the nineteenth-century drive for individual health and fitness was linked directly and explicitly to the desire to strengthen the nation as a body politic, the actual methods of transformation often drew—as they do today—on an ideology of the alternative or a belief that the ideal social state exists in opposition to the extant one. In the context of New Age capitalism, such an ideology turns eastward for its inspiration and relies on sentimentalism and nostalgia for a lost past in order to participate in contemporary cultural dialogues about modernity and antimodernity.

In this way, aromatherapy is said to originate in the aromatic practices and medicinals of ancient Egypt, Greece, and Rome, with possible connections to ancient Indian Ayurvedic practices and Chinese herbal medicine as well. Yet the portrayal of a deep connection with nature and the "intuition" that guided these ancient healers to the right plants are not unique to these past civilizations; they also apply to contemporary cultures that are believed to be closer to nature by virtue of their distance from Western centers of power and from Western cultural norms.[17] Thus, the Yawanawa, who live in the rainforests of western Brazil and who have entered into a partnership with the aromatherapy company Aveda, are associated with the peoples of ancient Egypt, Greece, Rome, India, and China. Similarly, the discourse of macrobiotic eating invokes ancient cultures—frequently unnamed but "since before the dawn of recorded history"[18]—as well as contemporary, but geographically remote, cultural groups like the Hunza of Kashmir or the Vilcabambans of the Ecuadorian Andes to align macrobiotics with an edenic past when people lived in harmony with nature and with each other. Not surprisingly, yoga and t'ai chi books and classes also romanticize the cultures and civilizations of their origins, transforming India and China from contemporary modern world economies to nations of spiritual peasants whose non-materialist goals are essentially to live in peace with nature and to seek enlightenment.

This type of seemingly benign and celebratory orientalism has a long legacy.[19] J. J. Clarke details the place of Eastern thought—particularly Buddhism, Taoism, Hinduism, and Confucianism—in Western intellectual traditions. He argues that orientalism must be understood as a complex and nuanced exchange as opposed to the more one-directional hegemony of imperialist dominance described by Edward Said.[20] For Clarke, the Western fascination with Eastern religions and philosophies represents a "counter-movement . . . which in various ways has often tended to subvert rather than confirm the discursive structures of imperial power."[21] Yet even such subversive counter-movements and cultural critiques—which are usually critiques of modernity—are deeply influenced by an orientalist logic. Clarke himself identifies the common tropes of popular orientalism which entangle the East in a romanticized past: the East as a timeless place that transcends the problems of this world, a place where the West can escape from its ills, a place where the West can seek peaceful solace.[22]

These themes are all echoed in a variety of familiar contexts ranging from nineteenth-century American transcendentalism to contemporary New Age philosophies. Contemporary New Age rhetoric—of which the discourses surrounding aromatherapy, macrobiotic eating, yoga, and t'ai chi are a fundamental part—with its emphasis on personal transformation on both bodily and spiritual levels can be understood as a reflexive reworking of this earlier transcendentalism. Seeking the key to health and happiness in ancient Eastern wisdom and ways extends these familiar nineteenth-century fascinations through the postmodern rhetoric of self-awareness and the contemporary political attention to global multiculturalism. The widespread and ironic acknowledgment of "reality" as a socially constructed pastiche together with a feel-good multiculturalism allows orientalist fascinations to pass for political correctness. Despite enduring similarities with nineteenth-century sensibilities, the American Way masquerades as cultural sensitivity.

Implicit in the turn to the East for spiritual guidance and social alternatives is a celebration of nature and the natural. Eastern cultures and thought have long been imagined and constructed as simplistically close to nature, and Clarke argues that this association plays out in a variety of Western philosophies and social movements from Nietzsche's nihilism and American transcendentalism to current environmental movements, many of which have explicitly invoked Eastern philosophies like Buddhism to support their causes.[23] The popular discourses of aromatherapy, macrobiotic eating, yoga, and t'ai chi operate in similar fashion. The romanticized lost past to which these bodily practices have been removed is itself an edenic one, a place of natural splendor and growth, free from the scars of modernity, and most important, located in the East—Egypt, Japan, India, China. In this way, orientalism and romanticization of nature collaborate to open up a space for the critique of modernity.[24]

The veneration of nature as a response to modernity has been best theorized by the German sociologist Ulrich Beck in his book *Risk Society*.[25] Beck argues that the successes of the modernizing process have been so great as to have introduced unanticipated risks in the form of side effects to the techno-industrial processes that sustain modernity.[26]

For Beck, risk society is a new type of social organization that is beginning to replace classic industrial society. In industrial society, the distribution of wealth is the dominant concern. In the transition from one model of society to the other, the typical hierarchy of distribution is gradually overturned, and those who generally have more access to wealth tend to be more protected from risk. However, as Beck notes, no one in risk society can be wholly safe from its dangers and poisons. Consequently, social responses to risk society—and to modernity—circle back to an imagined past existing prior to industrialization, a past epitomized by references to more integrated relationships with nature and the interconnectedness of all living things, especially as articulated in the environmental and peace movements.[27]

Here, again, planetary health is correlated with personal wellness. The popular conceptions of body and nature associated with aromatherapy products and macrobiotic diets as well as physical exercises like yoga and t'ai chi all exploit such anxieties about risk society and the diseases of modernity. As a result, the commodified forms of these bodily practices and their related products offer tangible ways of addressing both personal and planetary risks and wellness through the easy mode of consumption. Ultimately, the ideology of the alternative is a powerful form of popular orientalism that critiques modernity through the romanticization of nature, thus making for very attractive options in the global marketplace of New Age capitalism.

Alternative Health in Consumer Culture and Popular Discourse

The ideology of the alternative and the related promises of bodily and social transformation through "Eastern" practices are discussed and disseminated through a public sphere of alternative health. This public sphere can be imagined as a matrix of the various materials and modes of communication about alternative health and wellness that keep the practices and products in the public consciousness. In a sense, the public sphere is what feeds the fads.

The idea of a "public sphere" was first introduced by Jürgen Habermas, who sought to outline the relationship between public discourse and democratic action. For Habermas, the emergence of a public sphere—in the form of coffee-houses and salons—in the seventeenth century created a new social space for the rational-critical debates necessary for true participatory democracy. Habermas argues that the bourgeois participants of the seventeenth- and eighteenth-century public spheres were able to participate "rationally" in political discussion, while simultaneously bracketing individual identities and interests. For him, this exclusionary model of the ideal public sphere was then negatively transformed as the distinction between public and private began to deteriorate and "rational critical debate gave way to the consumption of culture."[28]

For Habermas, the public sphere is driven by communicative action[29] and thus political action is motivated by discourse—modes of social communication like rhetoric, images, and shared assumptions and beliefs that articulate a way of understanding the world. Expanding on Habermas' understanding of the relationship between communicative action and the public sphere, I propose that if the public sphere as we know it is further constituted by consumer culture—as is the case with the public sphere of alternative health—then participating in the related discourses and consumer behaviors is a form of communicative action. In this context, discourses and consumption are easily conflated to further promote the assumption that consumption itself can take the form of political action. (I discuss this phenomenon in detail in Chapter 5.)

Where the consumption of culture had detrimental effects on the ideal workings of the public sphere as Habermas theorizes it, consumer culture—advertising, brochures, catalogues, commercial products, popular "news" articles—is now largely responsible for generating the public sphere of alternative health and wellness. Indeed, the public sphere of alternative health depends on a global market based in New Age capitalism. The two are mutually constitutive. The consumer landscape and the processes by which alternative health practices become commodities generate opportunities for conveying the promise of a better way to live; in turn, the discourse of alternative health perpetuates the consumption of such goods and practices. I stress that this is a "global" market because of the ways in which the non-local origins of these practices and the products themselves are invoked as both ideological and practical selling points. Thus, popular alternative health practices like aromatherapy, macrobiotic eating, yoga, t'ai chi, and their related products exploit their associations—both real and imagined—with global, non-Western cultures. The increasing sense of global interconnectedness and an American desire for a feel-good multiculturalism have established a ready market for such commodified bits of difference.

Stuart Hall insightfully describes the sharp political dimension of this desire for commodified, but imagined, difference: global capitalism seeks to maintain impressions of difference through a type of cultural flattening that provides only the impression of particularities, thus extending the power of global capitalism by "operat[ing] through" and promoting various forms of cultural difference. Difference becomes a highly marketable commodity, and this form of globalization has made it chic "to eat fifteen different cuisines in any one week," to wonder at pluralism while taking "pleasure in the transgressive Other," to practice yoga and t'ai chi, even to consider the possibilities of macrobiotic eating once in a while. Similarly, just as the impression of difference enables the project of global capitalism, the impression of conservative resistance to such difference has precisely the same effect. As Hall suggests, capitalism is able to maintain its global dominance by presenting a world in which difference is commodified, sanitized, and thus *neutralized* for easy consumption: Global capitalism "is trying to constitute a world in which things are different. And that is the pleasure of it but the differences do not matter."[30]

Hall's cogent analysis of difference as a commodity emerges out of his understanding of the dialectic nature of the class struggle for control of cultural forces. He argues that popular culture ("the people's culture") is always marked by "the double movement of containment and resistance" as the dominant culture seeks to "disorganise and reorganise popular culture; to enclose and confine its definitions and form within a more inclusive range of dominant forms."[31] Ultimately, efforts to control cultural expressions and forms are played out in the marketplace where tradition and culture become historical processes in the broader context of class struggle. For Hall, tradition is a dynamic phenomenon[32] whose power exists in its inevitable recastings, in its ability to "take on new meaning and relevance,"[33] and it is this malleability that gives the term its cachet in the context of New Age capitalism.

In the public sphere of alternative health, "tradition" is invoked in the very ways that Hall is challenging. That is, tradition is assumed or imagined to be an unchanging, unbroken practice, and it is this assumption that makes the popular discourses of alternative health so persuasive. Thus, as I use the term, "traditionalization" refers to the processes by which third parties make cultural practices *seem* traditional, as though they were ancient customs that have been practiced continuously throughout the centuries and into the present in the various countries and cultural groups of their origins.

Ideology Incorporated: Consumption, Identity, and Ideology

It is through the interplay of public discourse and global markets that the nexus of personal, social, and planetary health is constructed and fixed in the public imagination and thus becomes more of an obligation than an option for individuals to pursue. That possibilities for alternative health and wellness seem to be everywhere is not a particularly radical observation, but the recent explosion of these offerings clearly warrants attention. This prevalence, in conjunction with the language of the marketplace, generates a sense of obligation to sample the various options until one finds the right practices for individual concerns.

The global marketplace foregrounds the life-enhancing qualities of these various bodily practices—overall wellness, preventative medicine, non-impact exercise, natural remedies for backaches, new beauty treatments, stress reduction, increased sensuality, more frequent relaxation. The public sphere of alternative health and wellness then disseminates the discourse. Together, they generate the obligation. Not only must we take responsibility for our own health, but we must take responsibility for social and planetary health as well. Because all the practices that could possibly fall within the category of alternative health and wellness are positioned as remedies for the ills of modernity and thus address social and planetary wellness, the individual is left with a sense of choice when deciding among options for alternative living. The very prevalence of the options, however, increases the obligation to experiment until the individual has found exactly those practices which work for him or her. The global marketplace maximizes the range by offering transcultural options that mix freely in their commodified forms. So, one can practice Chinese meditation while listening to Andean relaxation music and burning Indian incense. One can go on a yoga retreat in the Caribbean, enjoy aromatherapy massages, and eat a strictly macrobiotic diet based on Japanese foods. Through the very combination of the public sphere of alternative health and the global marketplace, the individual is empowered to create his or her own unique strategy for living in the modern world—at least according to an implicit code of consumption which suggests that buying into this bricolage is the first step toward responsibility.

What makes these new practices especially interesting is the extent to which the processes of traditionalization, commodification, and globalization work together on both ideological and practical levels. In consumer culture, identities become commodities to buy, and like other commodities, there are competing identities on the market. Traditionalization and commodification endeavor to create specific identities associated with the ideologies and bodily practices advanced in the public sphere of alternative health, identities which are eventually made available through purchase and affiliation with particular practices and goods. Such a process is at once social and individual. Insofar as a shared language of goods and symbols exists in advertisements and popular culture, the process is a social one and people can both signify and read the range of purchased identities through the outward display of goods. At the same time, the process is an individual and internal one as consumers buy into images and ideals which cohere with their own desire to take certain stances, their own desire to endorse or oppose the positions represented by the language of the commodity.

The idea that material goods can reveal something about their possessor's identity is not especially new or controversial.[34] What is arguable is the degree to which individuals have agency within consumer society. Those purchasing the practices and products at the core of the public sphere of alternative health likely believe in consumer agency because these practices and products are framed as alternative *purchasing* practices in addition to alternative health practices. Thus, for instance, buying certain lipsticks made by a company that reinvests its profits with indigenous peoples of the rainforest is a gesture in opposition to the production methods of more traditional cosmetic corporations who do not do this, and eating macrobiotically is a means of investing in organic farms and bypassing corporatized food production. In these small ways, consumers can believe that their purchases are also political acts that help subvert the larger systems of global capitalism. It is precisely this *impression* that consumer power has some ability to undermine capitalist systems, however, that ultimately allows New Age capitalism to profit and thrive.

This whole process is re-enacted by individual consumers in the context of New Age capitalism. Individuals can (re)create themselves as they desire, using consumption to their own ends. They may choose to complicate class distinctions or they may decide to subvert the social system as many countercultural movements often attempt to do. Along these lines, Rob Shields describes consumption as an active means of enacting a chosen lifestyle or social persona.[35] The consumer of the alternative practices and products described in this book, for instance, shows that she is an earth-friendly, socially responsible, enlightened global citizen in tune with herself, with nature, and with universal spirituality. This is where the little commodities like Om jewelry, Yoga Zone baseball caps, t'ai chi pants, and meals in macrobiotic restaurants serve their purpose in New Age identity construction. As Shields argues, individuals can use consumption to displace more traditional, socially structured, imposed identities by enacting various lifestyle choices such as these.

As Pierre Bourdieu has argued, however, aesthetic choices, cultural preferences, and cultural practices are all embedded in the *habitus*—the unconscious, taken-for-granted preferences that emerge through the individual's understanding of valid or appropriate tastes.[36] The idea of the *habitus* extends beyond a naturalized sense of judgment and manifests itself through the body.[37] Thus, class distinctions are conveyed through the body's physical attributes (height, weight, shape, posture) and its physical manners (ways of walking, sitting, eating, gesturing, speaking) which complicates the use of consumption as a means of enacting and signaling different social personae. Each social group has its own *habitus*. That is not to say that attempts to reproduce another group's habitus do not exist, however. In fact, this very desire for bodily mimesis, for a literal appropriation of another group's *habitus*, inspires many of the popular discourses around aromatherapy, macrobiotic eating, yoga, and t'ai chi. In essence, these discourses sell the possibility of exchanging one's own bodily status for another, higher one through the use of alternative practices that promise to reshape and rework the body.

Whether consumption allows consumers to remake themselves through their purchases depends in large part on the extent to which the language of goods is universally comprehensible within a mass culture like the United States. Shields and Bourdieu seem to argue that it is. And yet, as Malcolm Gladwell suggests, consumers also have the power to shift the social meaning of objects. As an example, he cites the case of young urban black men altering the meaning of Tommy Hilfiger clothing, which is expensive, designer, all-American preppy with a bent toward the nautical. Class implications should be clear from this description alone. Today, Tommy Hilfiger is the designer of choice among urban black America, a choice likely inspired by hip-hop music and culture. Gladwell also entertains the possibility that Tommy Hilfiger clothing has come to be a sign of hip-hop and rap, of urban black America, because of the multicultural designers who work with Hilfiger, a "forty-five-year-old white guy from Greenwich, Connecticut."[38] But such a proposition seems a bit unlikely as design teams are rarely known to consumers outside of the industry. In any case, through acts of consumption, urban black men appropriated Tommy Hilfiger clothing and charged it with a completely different set of identity associations and meanings.

Shifting the social meaning of Tommy Hilfiger clothing may be a form of social power for urban black men, but understanding the shift still depends on a social "language of goods" which is comprehensible across cultural divides. Such a language is what enables us to register the fact that urban black men have altered the meaning of Tommy Hilfiger clothing. In similar fashion, Grant McCracken suggests that the language of goods is so transparent to all members of society that it defuses any power that consumption may have for political or social protest. Ultimately, for McCracken, protest itself is simply an unintentional acknowledgment of the shared symbolic meaning of consumer goods, a statement that is comprehensible only through the larger cultural system.[39] For McCracken, the system is a closed one with no means of escape.

Of course, escape may not be the ultimate goal for those who attempt to mark themselves through acts of consumption. If the point is to use consumption to create differential identities and, to some extent, group affiliation as in the cases he suggests ("hippies," "punks," "gays," "feminists," "young republicans"), then the language of goods must be comprehensible across identity lines. After all, no identity makes sense without others to which it is compared. If the point is to use consumption as a means of protesting or altering the very system of consumption, however, then McCracken's contention that such acts of protest are constantly assimilated into the larger cultural system is likely to hold true.

The power of objects as cultural signs derives from the advertising (and implicit ideology) that accompanies them. In his semiotic discussion of objects and advertising, Jean Baudrillard stresses that it is not the object that we buy as a result of advertising; rather, we buy into the ideology of the advertisement. For Baudrillard, the success of advertising as political discourse exists in the distinction between *products* and *objects*, *products* being goods with social histories involving the people who actually participate in their making, whereas *objects* are cut off from such histories. Through advertising, which upholds the *object* and hides the *product*, the social reality of production and exploitation is hidden behind the conceptual image for sale.[40]

New Age capitalism relies on a widely comprehensible "language of goods" sustained by the ideological power of advertising. Without these, the consumption of alternative health practices and products and the discourses of alternative *purchasing* would make no sense. Despite the anti-materialist tenor associated with the public sphere of alternative health, the fact is that purchases reflect social status and class distinctions. Eating macrobiotically is expensive and time-consuming, and many of the celebrities who extol its virtues rely on full-time chefs to prepare their macrobiotic meals. Similarly, a membership at a large yoga studio like Yoga Zone costs over $1,000 annually, and even individual classes in smaller community centers range from $8 to $12. And the companies that invite yoga instructors to teach on-site tend to be Fortune 500 companies, not your local mom-and-pop store. The economic reality of pursuing these alternative health practices and buying these products necessarily makes them part of elite culture, and it is this association—in conjunction with the ideology of the alternative—that has made New Age capitalism so profitable.

McCracken's attempt to understand the intersection of ideology, consumption, and advertising through the psychologies of individual consumers provides a useful way of thinking about the relationship between consumption and New Age identity construction. McCracken draws on the psychological concept of displaced meaning to describe the ways in which commodities and consumption operate as individual and collective bridges to hopes and ideals. "Displaced meaning" is a process whereby cultural meaning "has been removed from the daily life of a community and relocated at a distant cultural domain."[41] Removing community (and/or personal) ideals to another space or time is a strategy for protecting them; thus, for instance, a community may constantly refer to a "glorious past," a time when the present community ideals are considered to have been more deeply integrated into community practices. Where New Age capitalism and alternative health are concerned, the ideals and values being mapped onto the "glorious past" are *imagined* desires and values, *imagined* values that suggest a prior community, all designed to counter some of the anxieties generated by postmodernity and by risk society.

McCracken argues that objects associated with ideal states of being—happiness, wealth, success, status, beauty—offer perfect sites for displaced meanings. Moreover, they serve this function best *before* they are actually purchased; anticipation, longing, and fantasy all precede ownership of the object and the imagined possession of the ideal state of being.[42] Possession is, of course, the danger. Once in possession of the object but without the corresponding change in status, beauty, or happiness, the individual becomes acutely aware of the disparity between the object as ideological symbol and the object as a means of personal transformation. One way out of such a dilemma is the perpetual displacement of meaning to yet other objects, thus ensuring an eternal quest for possession.

In general, the greater the distance, the greater the desire. And, somewhat ironically, desire and distance still intimate a closeness which maintains the desire.[43] As Georg Simmel suggests, desire for an object is measured by the extent of the sacrifice which an individual is willing to make in order to obtain the object. Desire and sacrifice converge in a cultural process of value determination. Because desire and sacrifice vary from person to person, value can never be objectively determined but emerges out of the exchange.

In the specific context of New Age capitalism, these ideas about consumer sacrifice and commodity value are translated into a language and an ideology of moral obligation and spiritual, at times even political, commitment. That is, financial sacrifice is rewarded with the cultural capital and moral sense of having consumed "responsibly"—whether that means responsibility toward one's own personal consciousness and spiritual development, one's community, or one's planet. In such an equation, the sacrifice—as enacted through consumption—makes public one's commitment to the loose conglomeration of New Age ideologies, a type of identity construction that draws directly on popular discourse as a way of literally embodying ideology and politics.

Because the global marketplace has made choice possible, consumers need not adhere to any single lifestyle—or identity—but can partake of the advantages of many. In this way, the ideological work implicit in the popular discourses of alternative health and wellness is partially containable through individual decisions about when, where, and for how long to consume. On the one hand, the individual has the ability to undermine the market's seeming dominance. On the other hand, consumer culture is expert in making us believe in that very sense of control through choices of consumption. Ultimately, it becomes a complex issue of personal belief and psychology.[44]

The Case Studies: Aromatherapy, Macrobiotic Eating, Yoga and T'ai Chi

The following three chapters draw on a range of popular materials to illustrate the ideological and political implications at the heart of New Age capitalism. Advertisements, popular books and magazines, promotional literature, travel brochures, product catalogues, instructional videos, and webpages are ubiquitous in large-scale, industrial, consumer societies like the United States. They are the materials of everyday life and often go unnoticed in our daily routines. From text to topic, from entertainment to art, they "have become the trivia of everyday life" that "saturate our social lives."[45]

As a result, collecting the data for the case studies involved actively participating in consumer society—roaming malls, bookstores, and the World Wide Web with my senses open to the seemingly endless ways in which these four particular practices are invoked and made available for purchase. It also involved writing for product catalogues and informational literature (following leads from advertisements in various magazines like *Yoga Journal* and *Vegetarian Times*), calling retreat organizers, clipping from hundreds of thousands of newspapers through the Lexis/Nexis database, and viewing yoga and t'ai chi videos. The sheer number of texts—product catalogues, free New Age publications, and newspaper and magazine articles—collected and passed along by friends and colleagues on a seemingly weekly basis testifies to the overwhelming presence of these discourses in our daily lives. While the public sphere of alternative health is also constituted by actual bodily practices and face-to-face discussion of these topics, I have limited this study to the commodified popular discourses of the three cases as a means of further investigating the undertheorized relationship between vernacular texts and ideology within the context of commodity culture. I am reading and analyzing the everyday texts of modernity as a way of understanding the particular ideologies of New Age capitalism as encoded in the language of alternative health and wellness.

Though the public sphere of alternative health at the center of this book is contemporary, and in many senses unique to modern life, similar public spheres of alternative health have existed throughout American history.[46] The following three chapters identify continuities of American preoccupations—with alternative health practices and dietary obsessions, with the promise of personal transformation, and with spiritual pursuits through Eastern philosophies. In drawing out the historical continuities of these recurring tropes and themes, I have tried to look to the past to push cultural studies into the future—beyond reflexivity for its own sake—to a place where it can exert a more politically engaged, activist force.

2

AROMATHERAPY

Aromatherapy as a traditional practice for holistic health has existed in its contemporary form since the early part of the twentieth century. Yet only in the past ten to fifteen years has it emerged with any force in consumer consciousness. What is said to have originated in ancient Egyptian unguents and Indian Ayurvedic practices has become the basis for aromatherapy in all of its commodified forms—holistic healing practices, essential oils for a range of uses, books for personal application, aroma lamps for refreshing rooms, and mass-produced scented products for bed and bath, body and psyche.

The popular discourses surrounding these aromatherapy products make clear the ideological work that occurs as practice is rendered product. The commodification of aromatherapy brings issues of gender, health, beauty, and sexuality to bear on issues of the environment, the health of the planet, medicine, and modernity. Through the extensive range and mainstream ubiquity of aromatherapy products, the personal is made political, and the individual is encouraged to assume greater responsibility for both through acts of consumption.

Origins of Aromatherapy and Essential Oils

The term "aromatherapy" was introduced in 1928 when the French chemist Dr. René-Maurice Gattefossé published a book entitled *Aromathérapie.* As the name suggests, aromatherapy is premised on the idea that floral and herbal scents can be used to cure a variety of physical, emotional, and spiritual maladies. All the fragrances used by aromatherapists are derived from the essential oils of flowers, herbs, trees, spices, and fruits. The scents are taken internally as well as applied through a variety of methods including inhalation, massage, and topical application.

Essential oils are the organic materials that give flowers, herbs, trees, spices, and fruits their fragrances. They exist in different areas of the plant, depending on the plant. For instance, the root is the source of essences like angelica and vetiver while flowers provide a wide variety of essences like rose, jasmine, and lavender. Most essences of herbs are found in the leaves, and the essences of many spices are found in the seeds. Essences of trees tend to exist in the woody portions (like sandalwood, cedarwood, and rosewood) as well as in the resins (like myrrh and benzoin). Fruit essences are commonly found in the skins, as is the case with all citrus fruits. The amount of essence in different varieties of plants might range from 0.01 percent to 10 percent, in some cases slightly more. In any case, it takes a large quantity of plant material to produce a very small quantity of essential oil. As an example, five and a half tons of rose petals yield only one pound of essential rose oil. In general, essential oils are extracted by mechanized steam distillation, though some require specialized processes like maceration in oil or mechanized pressing. Once extracted, the essential oils are highly concentrated, highly volatile, and quite unlike fatty oils; they tend to contain alcohols, esters, ketones, aldehydes, and terpenes which give them a more water-like consistency, though they are not water-soluble.

Because essential oils seem to capture and intensify the fleeting aroma of flowers, herbs, woods, and fruits, they have been described with a certain mystique, spirituality, magic, and romanticism. One leading aromatherapist describes essential oils as the plant's life force and spirit: "Essences are like the blood of a person. They are not the whole plant, but are whole, organic substances in themselves. Like blood they will die (lose their life force) if they are not properly preserved. . . . They are like the personality, or spirit, of the plant. The essence is the most ethereal and subtle part of the plant, and its therapeutic action takes place on a higher, more subtle level than that of the whole, organic plant, or its extract, having in general a much more pronounced effect on the mind and emotions than herbal medicine."[1] In naming the essential oil the plant's "life force" and "spirit," Robert B. Tisserand hints at the magical means by which aromatherapy effects its cures. Based on the principle of sympathetic magic, the plant's life force has the ability to influence the human life force; the "ethereal and subtle part of the plant" affects the individual on a "higher, more subtle level."

Susanne Fischer-Rizzi, another practicing aromatherapist and author of the popular *Complete Aromatherapy Handbook: Essential Oils for Radiant Health*, invokes even more fantastical imagery in describing essential oils: "To capture and store the fleeting scent of a flower—so as to have it available whenever you wish—has been desired since time began. How many wonderful memories and moods are tied to a particular scent! How often have we longed for the ability to capture the 'scent' of an experience so that we can let the 'genie out of the bottle' and relive those moments. That is magic—and we have succeeded!"[2] Like Tisserand, Fischer-Rizzi also associates essential oils with magic. In this case, however, the magic does not operate under any specific properties whereby "like affects like." Rather, Fischer-Rizzi's magic is an all pervasive one, a magic which grants essential oils and aromatherapy special powers which we need not even understand.

From Ancient Aromatics to Aromatherapy

The story of aromatherapy usually begins with the use of aromatics—any odiferous plant, tree, or part thereof—by ancient Egyptian, Greek, Roman, Indian, and Persian cultures.

The ancient Egyptians used aromatics in a variety of ways that extend far beyond the body itself.[3] Aromatic woods, and especially Lebanese cedars, were used in shipbuilding and in the construction of shrines, coffins, and boxes. Such woods were also used for more detailed, smaller items like dowels, handles, bricks, molds, paneling, and inlays. Aromatic gums and resins, particularly frankincense and myrrh, were the basic ingredients for incense, which was central to many religious rituals. At Heliopolis, the City of the Sun, three types of incense were burned in the daily worship of the Sun God Ra: at sunrise "resin" was burned; at noon, myrrh, and at sunset, the extravagant *kyphi*.[4] Kyphi was produced by mixing sixteen ingredients, including calamus, cassia, cinnamon, peppermint, citronella, pistacia, *convolvulvus scoparius*, juniper, acacia, henna, cyprus, "resin," myrrh, and even raisins. Kyphi was also used by the Greeks and the

Romans, and Plutarch contends that it had the power to "lull one to sleep, allay anxieties, and brighten dreams."[5]

The use of aromatics and perfumes also played a central role in Egyptian public life. During important occasions and festivals, perfuming could be quite elaborate, as exemplified by the indulgences offered up for an Alexandria parade sponsored by Egyptian king Ptolemy Philadelphus: "boys in purple tunics carrying frankincense, myrrh and saffron on golden dishes, a giant figure of Bacchus pouring out libations of wine, golden-winged images of Victory bearing incense burners, camels loaded down with spices, and innumerable floral decorations."[6]

The art and indulgence of public perfuming was not limited to ancient Egypt; the Romans and Greeks also practiced it widely. Roman theater stages were often sprinkled with saffron, and fountains at the amphitheaters frequently sprayed perfumed waters. Other grand events like athletic games also warranted lavish public perfuming. As part of the opening ceremonies for the games held by Antiochus Epiphanes, the king of Syria during the second century B.C.E., two hundred women went through the stands sprinkling everyone with perfume. During the games themselves, everyone who entered the gymnasium was sprinkled with essences of saffron, fenugreek, amaracus, or lilies, depending on the day.[7]

While the ancient Egyptian use of aromatics in construction, religion, and public life may have been creative and extensive, nothing compares to the ways in which they used aromatics to scent, decorate, heal, and mummify the body. Cosmetic boxes dating from the twelfth dynasty (c. 2000 B.C.E.) suggest that ancient Egyptians cared a great deal about decorating themselves. These cosmetic boxes are full of small pots and little jars made of stone which probably contained such standards as kohl, green eyeshadow, red ochre for coloring both lips and cheeks, and henna for staining the hands and fingernails. In addition, several pots likely held scented moisturizers for the hair and skin—unguents and ointments made of oils and animal fats. Aromatics were added to cosmetics to give them pleasant smells, and in the case of fats and oils used for moisturizers, to cover up the smell of the basic ingredients as they became rancid. Perfume jars containing unguents were discovered when the tomb of Tutankhamen was opened in 1922. The contents had solidified, but it was later determined that frankincense and "something resembling Indian spikenard" had been mixed into the base of animal fat.[8] Perfumes were extremely popular in ancient Egypt, and one common practice was for men to wear cones of solid unguent atop their heads as a means of perfuming themselves throughout the day. As the cone melted, their heads and bodies would be covered with perfume.

Aromatics and herbs were also used for medicinal purposes in ancient Egypt. They were often combined with other ingredients to create treatments, some to be taken internally while others were applied externally. Tisserand, a leading aromatherapist, cites two recipes from the Ebers Papyrus (18th Dynasty, c. 1580 B.C.E.), noting their similarity to contemporary aromatherapy treatments.[9] The Edwin Smith Surgical Papyrus contains similar prescriptions involving aromatics. For instance, a potion containing frankincense was prescribed for a woman with menstrual disorders as well as for a woman with an abscess in the breast.[10] Aromatics were also used for contraception, and one prescription involved inserting a mixture of acacia, coloquinte, dates, and honey in the vagina where it fermented into lactic acid, a known spermicide.[11]

The ancient Egyptians also relied on aromatics in death rituals and mummification. The body was prepared for burial by being washed and "sprinkled with a pungent mixture of water and dried leaves."[12] Aromatics also played a fundamental role in the funerary procession during which one individual dispensed perfume and another followed with a tray of burning incense. If the body were to be mummified, aromatics were added to the liquids for cleansing the abdominal and thoracic cavities as well as to mixtures for packing the body. After being cleansed and packed, the body was anointed with scented oils, most frequently cedar oil, and then rubbed with fragrant compounds. These mixtures were also applied to the bandages as the body was being wrapped. In general, the more thoroughly a corpse was embalmed with aromatic gums and spices, the more well-preserved it was, and this fact has led to contemporary uses of these aromatics for cosmetic applications and skin "rejuvenating agents."[13]

Like the ancient Egyptians, ancient Greek and Roman cultures also made extensive use of aromatics, in many cases imitating the perfumery and scenting practices of the Egyptians, Persians, and others in the East from whom they obtained many spices, gums, and other substances. Among the Greeks, fragrant woods like cypress, cedar, boxwood, and juniper were popular building materials, used for wainscoting, paneling, beams, and door pivots. The Greeks also added aromatics to inks and relied on them to disguise the foul odor of the tanneries where hides were worked into leather.

The ancient Greeks were indulgent with perfumes and aromatics, and the "gloriously heady blends"[14] were available in many forms—toilet waters, oils, dry powders, thick unguents, and incense. The wealthy even had their own perfumers who mixed individual scents for them. Both men and women enjoyed perfumes, and they often wore different scents on different parts of their bodies. Antiphanes describes one wealthy Greek's choice of scents: "[He] steeps his feet / And legs in rich Egyptian unguents; / His jaws and breasts he rubs with thick palm oil, / And both his arms with extracts of sweet mint; / His eyebrows and his hair with marjoram, / His knees and neck with essence of ground thyme."[15]

Not only did the Greeks have creative ways of scenting themselves, they also invented novel ways of scenting their houses and sharing perfumes with their guests, as was the custom among the well-to-do. One particularly innovative method of scenting a house involved drenching the wings of tamed birds with perfumes; the perfumes were disseminated throughout the house as the birds flew about. For banquets, fresh flowers might be strewn about the floor, and the table might be prepared by being rubbed with fresh mint leaves. Dinner guests were presented with fragrant garlands made from aromatic herbs and flowers such as roses, violets, hyacinths, apple blossoms, thyme, rosemary, myrtle, bay, and parsley. These garlands served the dual function of being both fragrant party favors and a means of counteracting the intoxicating effects of alcoholic fumes as they rose to the head. During the meal itself, guests were offered scented waters between courses for rinsing their fingers and then later presented with perfumed unguents with which to scent themselves. Even on relatively informal occasions, perfumes were customarily offered to the visitor.

In ancient Greece, the gods themselves were associated with particular fragrances and were believed to impart divine scents. For instance, Zeus, Demeter, and Aphrodite were said to bestow fragrances, delectable perfumes, and heavenly odors, and Mount Olympus was itself a "place of fragrance."[16] The sweet scent of the gods was most frequently attributed to the ambrosia and nectar upon which they feasted and with which they anointed themselves, though it was also believed that smoke from burnt offerings as well as offerings of fresh flowers and perfumes contributed to their heavenly odors.

The gods were also known to have created many aromatic plants, often as the result of their interactions with humans. For instance, in *Metamorphoses*, Ovid recounts a legend in which a king's daughter is seduced by the Sun and then killed by her father. Unable to revive the girl with his rays, the Sun sprinkles her body with fragrant nectar, promising that she shall still be able to travel up to him in the sky: "Straightaway the body, soaked with the celestial nectar, melted away and filled the earth around with its sweet fragrance. Then did a shrub of frankincense, with deep-driven roots, rise slowly through the soil."[17] As frankincense, the girl will forever rise to the sky in the form of incense and smoke. Similar aetiological legends exist for a variety of aromatic plants: myrrh was a woman who fell in love with her father; mint was Hades' spurned lover; laurel was born to Apollo's lover, a nymph. Cultural anthropologists studying the history of scent, Classen, Howes, and Synnott highlight the common theme of thwarted love in these legends and suggest that this theme ultimately bears on the religious significance of incense in ancient Greek culture. They argue that because these plants originate in thwarted love, they represent a "yearning for an unfulfilled union" which ultimately becomes an "implicit desire for union with the divine"[18] when the plants are burned and the fragrances are offered up to the gods.

Divine origin also enhanced the medicinal powers of aromatics, and a number of recipes for aromatic medicines are inscribed on marble tablets in the temples of Aesculapius and Aphrodite. Aesculapius was a Greek god of healing, born to Apollo and a nymph at Epidauros, a city that later became known for its health spas, baths, and healing centers. Priestesses at the temple of Aesculapius dispensed "healing essences" which were said to compete successfully with the treatments prescribed by the apothecaries. Among the most celebrated cures from this time comes from the story of Milto, the daughter of a poor Greek artisan. Every morning Milto went to Aphrodite's temple with garlands of fresh flowers as offerings, her poverty preventing her from making more expensive ones. She was a very beautiful young woman, but soon she began to develop a large tumor on her chin. One night Aphrodite came to her in a dream and told her to apply some of the roses from her altar to her chin. After Milto followed the goddess' instructions, the tumor receded, her beauty shone forth, and she eventually "sat on the Persian throne as the favourite wife of Cyrus."[19]

Whether dispensed by priestesses at the temple of Aesculapius or by physicians and perfumers, aromatics were widely used for medicinal purposes. The ancient Greeks believed that the very scents of aromatics, whether inhaled or absorbed directly into the skin, contained healing powers. Thus, as mentioned earlier, wearing fresh flower garlands on the head during banquets was thought to stave off the effects of excessive drinking. The physician Philonides advocated the use of garlands and perfumes for general good health as well as for specific ailments. He claimed that rose garlands alleviated headaches and cooled the body while myrtle garlands were particularly effective stimulants and counteracted drunkenness.[20] Perfumes and aromatics, often mixed with wine to produce lotions and ointments, were also applied directly to burns, inflammations, and open wounds. Other aromatic remedies included saffron to treat lunatics, incense and the oil of rose to relieve swelling of the breasts, rosemary and anemone leaves to promote milk secretion, and gum mixed with honeyed vinegar to treat toothaches and obesity. To this knowledge of specific remedies, the Greek physician Maresthueus added information about the general properties of many aromatic flowers. He discovered that the scents of different flowers seemed to have either stimulating or sedative properties: for instance, rose and hyacinth were invigorating and refreshing, while lily and narcissus were oppressive and likely to cause drowsiness if inhaled in large quantities.[21]

Like the Egyptians, the ancient Greeks also used aromatics in death preparations and funerary rituals. After being washed, the body of the deceased was anointed with aromatic oils and a garland of fresh flowers was placed on the head. Fresh flowers were also strewn about the couch where the corpse was laid out. After a period of mourning, the body was placed in a casket, frequently made of cypress, and buried. After the funeral, the house and the family and friends of the deceased were purified by the burning of incense.

The Roman use of aromatics was very similar to that of the ancient Greeks. Aromatics were featured prominently in everything from construction, cooking, and cosmetics to medicine and religion. Perhaps the most well-known use of aromatics involves the famed Roman baths. The process of bathing began with a sweat in the *sudatorium* (akin to a steam sauna), followed by a warm bath in the *tepidarium*, and then a cool swim in the *frigidarium*. From there, those who could afford it proceeded to the *unctuarium* where they were massaged and anointed with perfumes and fragrant oils. However, the sweet fragrances associated with the baths were not exclusive to those who could afford the unctuarium; in some cases, even the baths and pools were perfumed. Among wealthy Romans, there was no end to the perfuming, and even domestic animals were frequently perfumed with their owners' favorite scents.

Medicinally, the Romans were strongly influenced by the Greeks in their use of aromatics for healing. Perhaps the most thorough compendium of ancient Roman aromatic cures is Pliny's *Natural History*,[22] which is probably a recorded reflection of the folk medicine current during his time. Similar recipes also exist for more cosmetic healing like the removal of blemishes from the skin as well as for more general cosmetic applications like facial masks.

In general, the authors of aromatherapy books tend to agree about the ancient Egyptian, Greek, and Roman "origins" of aromatherapy. However, the story of Palestinian, Arab, Indian, and Chinese influences is much less thoroughly recorded and much less consistent. The use of aromatics by the Palestinians was very similar to that of the ancient Egyptians, Greeks, and Romans,[23] but few present this history as part of the story of aromatherapy. Some link aromatherapy with the classical Indian *Ayurvedas*, even if only remotely related. The *Ayurvedas* are sacred texts of herbal medicine (c. 2000 B.C.E.) and the basis of a holistic health system which is still practiced today. Though a system of herbal medicine, the *Ayurvedas* do include a number of preparations involving aromatic essences, and thus many consider Ayurvedic medicine to be related to aromatherapy. Others include Chinese herbal medicine as part of the history of aromatherapy, in particular Emperor Shen Nung's *Great Herbal* (*Pen Tsao*) (c. 1000-700 B.C.E.), a compendium of approximately 350 medicinal plants and remedies. In addition, Chinese alchemists were believed to have experimented with plant perfumes and essences in their search for immortality. The Real Goods catalogue for environmentally conscious products even refers to Native American aromatherapy: "Aromatherapy candles create a kaleidoscope of color and light. Kaleidoscope aromatherapy candles are based on the Native American belief that fragrance can elicit the body's self-healing powers."[24]

Of course, the history of aromatics is not the history of aromatherapy. The ancient Egyptians, Greeks, and Romans may have used a number of different essential oils, but for the most part their use of aromatics involved other parts of the plant and often relied on much more than just the plant's scent. Yet the consistency of the story which traces the "origins" of aromatherapy to the ancient use of aromatics is remarkable: a survey of twenty-five popular aromatherapy books indicates that 80 percent present this history. Moreover, of the five that did not refer to this history, only one included any history at all.

The force of this particular story derives from a more general trend toward the past, a celebration and romanticization of "purer" or "simpler" times when people were believed to be more attuned to nature, more spiritual, more fulfilled. The popularity of various New Age practices and beliefs and the superficial attention to indigenous peoples all over the world (despite their frequent exploitation in global systems of production and exchange) attest to the breadth of this trend. The identification of aromatherapy with the ancient use of aromatics is part of an attempt to counter modernity and the techno-industrial capitalist system it signifies. Tisserand opens his *Art of Aromatherapy*, a "classic" text intended for a popular audience, by recounting the social ills of modernity, in this case modernity being the moment when art and science were rendered different:

> At one time there was no distinction between science and art, between knowledge and ability. . . . As we have split knowledge into art and science, science has become more powerful, more predominant. At first sight it seems practical, and indeed it is, to have telephones, computers, televisions, and so on. But, like a child with a new toy, we misuse our abilities; we do not know how to restrain or control such things, or put them to the uses for which they were created. Instead they become instruments with which to spread suffering—war, political bias, economic disaster. . . . We have arrived at the point

where money, power, and scientific fact have become ends in themselves, instead of means to bring about a more comfortable, peaceful, and happy life.[25]

Here, the icons of modernity—telephones, computers, televisions, money—are also the very sources of the suffering from which we seek to escape. The power of science has delivered us to a place far from the romanticized life of antiquity where science was more of an art, a knowledge based on "intuition." Implicit in this discussion, of course, is the notion that aromatherapy (and similar lifestyle changes) can help us overcome the ills of modernity by helping us recapture that past where people "had a deep love of nature and respect for plants, and in some ways seemed to understand them better than we do today."[26] Tisserand seems to suggest that this past was a kinder, gentler one where wars, political biases, economic disaster, money, power, and science did not wreak havoc on the people. Thus, it is not surprising that he fails to mention any such suffering in his history of aromatherapy, though ancient history is at least as well known for these types of political intrigue as for its use of aromatherapy. In fact, aromatics were frequently used to treat—or at least to disguise the odor of—wounds suffered during battle.[27]

Those whose knowledge predated "science" somehow relied on an instinctive understanding of nature, undoubtedly the result of a more spiritual relationship with the environment. Tisserand underscores this distinction in his description of the "herbalists of previous centuries" whom he suggests had just this type of knowledge of plants and healing: "They knew where to find their plants growing naturally. They knew in which season and at what time of day to pick them; which planets ruled them, and how this affected their properties. They knew virtually nothing of the chemical constituents of the herbs, or why they had certain properties. But they knew a little about disease, and knew which herbs were good for certain ailments. This knowledge was based on no kind of science, except that of trial and error, added to the experience of their predecessors and, perhaps more significantly, to their own intuition."[28] According to Tisserand, these ancient herbalists had a natural sense of botany, astrology, and healing, an innate understanding which he calls "intuition," and it is this sense which he pits against "science." After all, their knowledge was "based on no kind of science." Tisserand never makes clear the difference between "science" and "trial and error" and "the experience of their predecessors," which sound vaguely like the methods of experimentation upon which much "scientific" research is based.

In similar fashion, another aromatherapist emphasizes the ancient Egyptians' instinctive knowledge of aromatherapy, linking it with the fulfillment of basic human needs: aromatherapy "has always been bound up with two of humankind's most basic needs—our dependence on plants for food and medicine, and the expression of our spiritual selves. Perhaps no other culture understood the interrelationship of these two aspects better than the ancient Egyptians. For them, the magic and mystery of aromatherapy permeated the whole of their daily existence."[29] In this case, instinct—"the magic and mystery of aromatherapy"—is more completely differentiated from its implied opposite—science—and spirituality is again invoked to signal the purity and righteousness of the past.

Aromatherapy and the Ideology of the Alternative

Through this discourse of nature and spirituality, these aromatherapists create a lost past, a fragrant eden drastically different from our modern world of war, political bias, and economic disaster. Aromatherapy provides a way of living according to this past, and it is in this sense that the practices and products of aromatherapy are part of an "alternative" lifestyle and an alternative to modernity. Thus, aromatherapists advocate more than aromatherapy. As Tisserand states: "Aromatherapy cannot be divorced from a number of things: the basic principles of natural therapeutics, massage, diet, and our whole attitude to life. . . . These principles are complementary, and are based on man's interpretation of nature from his understanding of life. . . . Surely the universe was created and is sustained by one set of principles, so there can only be one truth. . . . The main principles of our therapy are Life force, Yin-yang, [and] Organic foods."[30] In keeping with his thorough celebration of the past, Tisserand represents this alternative lifestyle with an aura of spirituality and a fundamental understanding of nature. Moreover, he grants "our therapy" the status of universal truth, and it's difficult to argue with that.

Hasnain Walji presents a similar, though slightly less ardent, approach in *The Healing Power of Aromatherapy: The Enlightened Person's Guide to the Physical, Emotional, and Spiritual Benefits of Essential Oils*. He, too, emphasizes the importance of an alternative lifestyle as the best way of approaching health holistically. Holistic health is premised on the understanding that an individual is influenced by the body, mind, and soul and that none works in isolation of the others. Thus, health is not so much the absence of disease but a "positive state of well-being in which all the different elements that make up an individual are in balance and working in harmony with each other."[31] To achieve this positive state of well-being, Walji advocates a nutrient-rich organic diet, exercise, and mental relaxation as well as aromatherapy for maintaining (or achieving) physical, emotional, and spiritual health.

The holistic approach to health seeks to rectify the classic Cartesian dualism between mind and body. Whereas Western medicine tends to address specific ailments by focusing on the individual body parts involved, holistic medicine attempts to identify a cure by addressing the underlying reasons for an illness: "The holistic practitioner will look for the meaning behind the illness. What are these symptoms saying about the individual? What does he want out of his life that he isn't getting? What is his attitude toward life? Are there recurring patterns in his illnesses? Has there been a major life change that renders him emotionally, and therefore physically, more vulnerable to attack?"[32] Theoretically, this seems like an ideal approach to health; however, identifying these underlying causes of illness is likely to be more difficult than asking the patient this series of questions.

Aromatherapy is said to operate on a truly holistic level, restoring health and happiness for everyone regardless of the particular complaint. Fischer-Rizzi describes the way in which essential oils help people achieve holistic health and happiness:

> The number of unhappy people in our society has grown steadily—we know that inner emptiness cannot be filled by external prosperity or diversion. And maybe that's why we are "ready" now for these long neglected healing methods—the pure essential oils—the concentrated fragrant components of plants and herbs that may benefit everyone. . . . Aromatherapy acts in accordance with holistic principles: it awakens and strengthens vital energies and self-healing capabilities of the patient. . . . In addition, essential oils invite one

to appreciate the beauty and wonders of creation, providing us inner contentment. As a gate to our soul, essential oils give us the impetus to search for meaning in our lives.[33]

Indeed, aromatherapy sounds like a miracle cure. Inner peace and personal contentment are available in little bottles of essential oils, and they smell good too.

And yet, the antidote for the "inner emptiness" that Fischer-Rizzi claims "cannot be filled by external prosperity" requires external prosperity to be acquired. The sale of aromatherapy products is estimated to be $300-500 million, with an annual growth rate of approximately 30 percent.[34] Individual products range from Bath & Body Works' $3.50 bars of aromatherapy thyme soap and $5 linen sprays all the way up to Aveda's $830-per-ounce violet absolute.[35] Several independent essential oil and affiliated product suppliers attribute the size and growth of the aromatherapy market to more general interests in alternative therapies and to an increase in overall life stresses.[36] Whether increases in life stress are real or imagined or created to sell products, a wide range of retail outlets and mail-order businesses are rising to meet the demand—or to collectively generate consumer need—for aromatherapy products. Even clothing stores like the Gap, the Limited, Eddie Bauer, Urban Outfitters, and Banana Republic, as well as variety stores like Pier 1 Imports, the Nature Company, and Hallmark Cards, have introduced aromatherapy and body care lines with names that evoke the soothing effects of aromatherapy like "bliss," "calm," "relax," and "quiet."

While aromatherapists may promise the natural fragrances of holistic contentment, however, the process whereby New Age capitalism transforms aromatherapy practices into a collection of products ultimately fragments the body into a series of parts and separates the mind and soul into various states of being, each "treatable" with different aromatherapy products like lip glosses and hair conditioners, foot lotions for pedicures and hand treatments for manicures. Emotional states and psychological moods are similarly categorized and thus controllable. For instance, Bath & Body Works, the nation's leading retailer of bath products, offers four primary therapies—Pure Refreshment, Tranquil Sleep, A Little Romance, and Stress Release—in a wide variety of applications for body and home. Among the options are a thyme bar soap ($3), concentrated home fragrance spray ($4), linen spray ($5), scent-filled candle ($12), bath and shower gel ($8.50), massage lotion ($9), body lotion ($10), mineral bath salts ($10), and "pulse point cream" ($10). For the slightly more curious, Bath & Body Works also offers oil essence samplers in Sweet Dreams and Stress Less "scents" ($12 for two 0.5 oz. oil es-sences), as well as several individual oil essences ($8.50). (Oil essences are not to be mistaken for essential oils. Essential oils are the pure essence extracted from plant materials, and oil essences generally consist of some sort of oil base with a few drops of essential oil.) The Bath & Body Works products promise to manipulate individual moods and psychological conditions rather than provide Fischer-Rizzi's "inner contentment" or personal fulfillment, though the product description for the Pure Refreshment linen spray contends that its combination of sandalwood and citrus essential oils provides "a natural way to revive [one's] own spirits."[37]

Of course, Bath & Body Works is not the only bath and body store to carry aromatherapy products: national and international retailers like Aveda, the Body Shop, Bare Escentuals, Garden Botanika, and H_2O, as well as local independents like Body Time in Berkeley, California, all have aromatherapy product lines. And with the 1997 introduction of Coty's aromatherapy line, even pharmacies and drugstores are able to carry the products. Coty's Healing Garden line is carefully positioned near the pharmacy both to emphasize its status as an alternative health system and to distinguish it from other fragrance and bath products.[38] Like Bath & Body Works, Coty spins products off of four primary fragrance therapies—Lavender Therapy for relaxation, Green Tea Therapy for enlightenment, Jasmine Therapy for sensuality, and Tangerine Therapy for energy.[39] The thirty-nine related products include room sprays, body soaps and lotions, cologne sprays, candles, dried flowers, and incense.[40] Again, each of the four fragrance categories targets a specific mood or state of being rather than inspiring some sort of overall contentment.

The proliferation of spin-off fragrance therapies exemplifies the capitalist necessity to divide the product line as well as the body and mind and spirit into as many parts as possible to ensure a continually growing market and consumer base. This type of serialization and innovation has helped Bath & Body Works dominate the market in the past five years; approximately 30 percent of the chain's products are new each season.[41] As Beth Pritchard, CEO of Bath & Body

Works, points out, however, innovation is only one way to expand the business: "Because you don't desperately need our products, we must entertain you. It's a Disney mentality."[42] And, at this mass market level, it is the Disney triad of entertainment, packaging, and imagery that's being sold. Innovation and entertainment depend on the creation of new consumer needs as well as the creation of new remedies for old consumer needs. Thus, product lines like those owned by Bath & Body Works and Coty remind consumers of the stress or lack of romance in their lives, and for those who don't even realize that they have stressful, bland lives, the products are here to acquaint them with all of the new possibilities for happiness. In similar fashion, prepackaged aromatherapy treatments exist for more common conditions. Among the pre-packaged aromatherapy kits available at Borders Books in Philadelphia are the Hangover Pack, the Insomnia Pack, the Stress Pack, and the Headache Pack. Each pack ($16.95) contains a remedy booklet, two bottles of pure essential oils (approximately eight drops each), and a massage oil for mixing the remedies. Pritchard's "Disney mentality" is particularly clear in the packaging and design of these aromatherapy kits, which are more likely to be purchased as novelties or gifts than as alternative treatments.

Even the books written by aromatherapists consider the body part by part and the psyche state by state. For instance, Tisserand provides a "therapeutic index" for determining the best essential oils for specific conditions,[43] listing essential oils for treating ailments related to major organs like the heart, the liver, the appendix, the kidneys, and the gall bladder. He also provides remedies for a number of emotional states like anxiety, depression, frigidity, mental fatigue, nervous tension, and vertigo. In private practice, aromatherapists may treat individuals holistically to address specific problems like those of the liver or the kidneys; however, in their books, they break down this holistic approach by discussing the use of essential oils with respect to individual body parts and emotional conditions. This disjuncture between aromatherapy as a practice and aromatherapy as a product underscores the functional futility of searching for a way to unify mind, body, and soul in the midst of consumer culture and New Age capitalism.

In addition to being presented as a holistic approach to wellness in general, aromatherapy is also positioned as a natural alternative to Western medical practices in particular. While all of the books and products establish clear disclaimers so as not to be mistaken for medical texts, they give the impression of being alternative forms of such. Fischer-Rizzi opens her section on healing with essential oils in precisely this manner: "Many of us have become concerned about the side effects of chemically produced medications. We know that they undermine our bodies' innate self-healing processes, and many of us have tried to reduce our dependence on such prescriptions . . . essential oils, properly administered, produce no harmful side effects. On the contrary, unlike chemotherapy, they mobilize the body's own self-healing powers."[44] Again, aromatherapy is coded as "natural" in opposition to the "chemically produced medications" of Wester medicine. As a natural source of healing, aromatherapy also restores wellness by compensating for the damage done by these representatives of "modern" medicine, drugs and prescriptions which "undermine our bodies' innate self-healing processes" and encourage chemical dependencies.

This idea that the medical successes of modernization introduce attendant bodily hazards has been theorized more generally by Beck in his consideration of risk society. Beck argues that in such a society, concerns about the distribution of risks replace the concerns about the distribution of wealth that exist in classical industrial society. Thus, where *equality* is the ideal paradigm for industrial society, *safety* becomes the ideal for risk society. Within such a context, social activists fight for protection from the risks of modernization, risks which threaten the safety, health, and viability of all living things, including the earth itself. Beck contends that as the risk society continues to develop, the public is divided into two general camps, one predicated on scientific rationality, the other on social rationality, and the two sides "talk past each other."[45] Given the deeply entrenched scientific bias in Western societies, the division between social rationality (as expressed through social movements) and scientific rationality is not simply a divide between public citizen and professional scientist. Rather, the scientific paradigms are so extensive and dominant as to have become naturalized; thus, it is those social movements which resist the hegemony of science and modernization that constitute the "alternative."

Risk society thrives on a discourse of individual responsibility. Individuals are encouraged to take personal responsibility for righting the wrongs developed in conjunction with the technological and medical successes of modernization. Global concerns about the viability of the planet as well as individual concerns about personal health all fall to the individual, often—ironically—because the problems are presented as too enormous or too costly for governmental institutions and businesses to rectify. The discourse surrounding aromatherapy addresses the concerns of risk society on two fundamental levels. As an alternative to Western medical treatments, aromatherapy provides a nonchemical, holistic system for treating disease and wellness. At the same time, because aromatherapy involves the sustainable use of plants and plant products (often organically grown), it contributes to the protection of the environment and to the earth's botanical resources.

Thus, Fischer-Rizzi's positioning of aromatherapy in contrast to Western scientific medicine typifies the way responsibility is individualized in risk society. Her claim that "we want to assume more responsibility for our own well-being and to concentrate on preventing illness in the first place"[46] might as well be a mantra for those who hope to counteract the risks of modernization. Tisserand echoes this point in his explicit contrast between aromatherapy and drug therapies administered by medical doctors: "If you have influenza, and your doctor gives you an antibiotic, all he is doing is perhaps speeding your recovery by a day or two; you do not really need that antibiotic. And there is a growing and real problem with antibiotics. Because of their indiscriminate use, bacteria are becoming resistant to them. New strains appear, and new drugs have to be manufactured. It is a race which, once we have entered it, we can never quit, and it has no foreseeable end."[47] Here, Tisserand touches on the various themes invoked to justify aromatherapy as an ideal way of countering the bodily poisons of risk society—the dangers of chemical drugs, the mistaken beliefs of the medical establishment, the potential dependence upon science, medicine, and chemicals.

The commodification of aromatherapy furthers the principle of individual responsibility as different products encourage consumers to take control of different body parts and different emotional states, even different situations. The overwhelming numbers and types of oils, lotions, creams, hydrating sprays, balms, wraps, steams, bath salts, room sprays, linen sprays, candles, and incense require a range of diversified effects to justify their existence. Thus, consumers are encouraged to use weekly aromatherapy facial masks which promise a deep moisturizing and a tightening of the skin to prevent signs of aging. For daily moisturizing, they may use a hydrating spray which provides a light refreshing way of moisturizing the face in the morning and a heavier alpha-hydroxy cream for the night. In addition, there are aromatherapy products for steaming and opening clogged pores and for exfoliating dead skin cells, thereby allowing the healthy skin to shine forth. There are special astringents and toners, some for special times of the day when the face is said to need a different level of refreshing or oil-removal, and special treatments and packs for acne. Of course, the products all complement each other, and the conscientious consumer who really cares about his or her face will use all of them, in the proper fashion, at the proper time, on the proper day.

The integration of such products into a complete system grants the consumer a sense of control over his or her beauty and implies a certain individual responsibility for it. And this is just the face. The same systematic approach applies to hair, body, skin (different parts require different products, naturally), hands, feet, nails, and elbows, not to mention emotions and moods. Products like Bath & Body Works' A Little Romance and Coty's Jasmine Therapy for enhancing sensuality put the responsibility of romance and sensuality in the consumer's hands (or nostrils or bath water or bed linens). When considered together, the very range and depth of aromatherapy products suggest the possibility of perfection through essential oils. One can live a life of relaxation and energy with no stress while enjoying tranquil sleep and sensuous romance, even enlightenment and perfect beauty, through the aid of an aromatherapy product line. New Age capitalism presents all of the possibilities for perfection. It is the consumer's responsibility to take advantage of them.

As noted earlier, aromatherapy also addresses risk society's concern for the viability and health of the planet. Though essential oils range in quality, the finest derive from wild and/or organically grown botanicals.[48] In turn, aromatherapy as a whole benefits from this association with organic flowers and plant essences and enjoys quite a reputation for being an environmentally conscious industry. The exact ways in which aromatherapy protects the planet from demise, however, are unclear. Everyone from aromatherapists to essential oil suppliers and aroma researchers praises the earth-friendly nature of aromatherapy, but no one articulates the precise nature of its environmentalism. Rather, "aromatherapy has jumped on the bandwagon of the 'save the earth' green movement"[49] and insinuated itself in popular discourse and public consciousness as a logical rider. The association seems as simple as plants=green=earth-friendly.

Whatever the reasons for the association between aromatherapy and the green movement, those who sell aromatherapy products are taking advantage of its eco-friendly reputation. In fact, "green consumerism" has inspired a worldwide increase in essential oil production and created markets for new aromatherapy products: "In response to the unusual demands of 'green' consumerism, the structure and nature of the fragrance/flavor industry have undergone rather remarkable change. Opening up are new worldwide markets for growers and distillers of small and large volume essential oils and other aromatic botanicals. . . . Environmental home fragrances, sophisticated skin care products, and those for therapeutic massage are stimulating a growing range of psychological applications, mood fragrances, and therapeutic massages."[50] Perhaps the world's foremost expert in combining environmentalism with the aromatherapy business is Aveda's Horst Rechelbacher. Rechelbacher is largely responsible for introducing the term "aromatherapy"—as well as its principles—to the American public in 1978 when he started the haircare and cosmetic company Aveda. Since then, he has established an international aromatherapy empire on the foundation that aromatherapy is healthy for both the individual and the planet.

Others have followed Rechelbacher's flower-strewn path and developed major cosmetic corporations on the principles of aromatherapy and the use of natural ingredients. For instance, Origins Natural Resources, the smallest and newest of the Estée Lauder cosmetic companies, has taken its aromatherapy line to the top of department store sales. As with Aveda, Origins attributes the popularity of its product line to the fact that its principles, practices, and products resonate with the risk society's anxiety over personal and planetary wellness: "Origins . . . is tapping into late 20th century concerns about quality of life and the environment. The name alone is intended to suggest a happier, more innocent era when humanity was in touch with its roots."[51] As with the frequently invoked history of aromatherapy, the reference to—and nostalgia for—an earlier era predating the risks of modernity underscores the power of aromatherapy as an antidote to the ills of modernity. The celebration of aromatherapy as a way of combating damage to the earth and to the environment is unbelievably widespread. Even Disney seizes upon this connection in its attempts at "environmentally responsible tourism" with its "all natural aromatherapy blend of in-room guest amenities called Eco Care."[52] Disney is much more explicit in naming its aromatherapy products than anyone else. There is no question as to whom and what benefits from Eco Care aromatherapy.

Ultimately, risk society provides a wealth of advertising material for those who market aromatherapy products while simultaneously priming consumers for their necessity. At the same time, the transformation of aromatherapy practices into products opens up a forum for a much more extensive range of social discourse about risk and responsibility. Because the risks of modernity are largely indiscernible to the senses, the popular messages surrounding aromatherapy and risk society fashion themselves as public service announcements. Unlike the sensory-assaulting pollutants and hazards of earlier eras, "the risks of civilization today typically escape perception and are localized in the sphere of physical and chemical formulas (e.g., toxins in foodstuffs or the nuclear threat)."[53] In general, our daily lives tend to be free from the taste of contaminants in our foods, free from the feel of toxins damaging our skin, free from the bodily understanding of immune systems compromised by too many antibiotics, and that very invisibility inspires the greatest anxiety. Information passed through product packages and in-store displays assumes an educational quality, an almost conspiratorial sharing of the "facts" which will allow the consumer to counteract and prevent some of the risks of living in a modern industrial society. As aromatherapy moves from practice to product, discussions about its personal and ecological benefits move from immediate face-to-face conversations to the more permanent product labels and packages, store displays and signage, product descriptions in catalogues and product reviews in popular literature as well as all other imaginable spaces of consumer society.

Coty's marketing strategy for its new Healing Garden line of "holistic aromatherapy products" exemplifies the way in which risk society and consumer society converge to create a self-perpetuating cycle of risk and counter-risk. For those not already familiar with the advantages of aromatherapy, Coty created revolving floorstands—"designed to let customers shop it from every angle"—which offer testers as well as information explaining the products and their various therapeutic benefits.[54] In addition, Coty's advertising strategy calls for an all-print campaign to ensure that the company has ample space to explain fully the concepts behind the Healing Garden. Terry Siegel, Coty's senior marketing director, touches on the ideas explained through the print campaign and justifies the $5.6 million expenditure: "This is beyond fragrance and bath and body, although some retailers will merchandise it in fragrances or in bath. This is really a whole different arena. It goes into stress reduction, into relaxation, into energizing the body. It goes into the home environment with candles and dried florals and incense sticks. It is responding to what is now a major trend throughout the country, with people so stressed out that it's become an epidemic. . . . We need an intimate setting, and we need time to explain the concept. We believe it's better to do four-page supplements than 30-second commercials."[55] Here, Coty reorients Beck's "social rationality"—typically confined to fairly educated social activists—to the mass market of drugstore and pharmacy shoppers, the consumers at the foundation of New Age capitalism.

In similar fashion, Bath & Body Works uses in-store displays and signs to "educate" the consumer about the aromatherapeutic value of their products. One small sign in the middle of a display in a Philadelphia store in July 1997 read: "The Beads Make it Better. New! Aromatherapy Body Care. With tiny beads of real essential oils to help you relax, refresh and unwind." Surrounding the sign are bottles of Bath & Shower Gel, the little beads of essential oil aglitter and suspended within the colored gels.

Another popular site for educating the consumer is the package itself. Bath & Body Works sells samplers of different remedies (with names such as Stress Relief and Tranquil Sleep) which are primarily packaging—6 by 9 1/2-inch rectangular cardboard sleeves with cutouts in front to reveal the contents, what appear to be miniature bottles of the body lotion, bath and shower gel, the massage lotion, and the mineral bath salts. Once out of the cardboard, however, it becomes apparent that the "bottles" are actually just shapes molded in a single 6 by 9 1/2-inch piece of plastic. Releasing the lotions or gels or salts is easy with a simple snip of the scissors. Though the package promises of the bath salts that "just half a packet in a tub of running water will help soak away your troubles," it is impossible to close up the plastic nonbottle in order to save the remaining half for a second bath.

Product test marketing probably helped Bath & Body Works choose green for its line of Stress Relief products, and in this case the color seems to reinforce the idea that aromatherapy products are natural and good for the environment; this package even reminds the consumer that the finished products are not tested on animals. Of course, it says nothing about the large piece of plastic used to give the impression of individual bottles.

The psychology and politics of the package aside, the large back surface offers ample space for teaching the consumer about the specific benefits to body and soul inspired by the use of the chosen essential oils. For instance, behind the "bottle" of bath and shower gel, the package reads: "Burdock and chamomile gently cleanse skin and micro-beads of essential oils release a calming scent to help wash away tensions."

In essence, the commodification of aromatherapy has made possible the product turnstiles, the package surfaces, and the print advertisements necessary to sustain itself. In addition, as Beck argues, risk society makes possible new markets and alters the very concept of need until it brings about a self-referential economy, an economy which generates imagined needs to fuel a system that depends not so much on meeting human needs as on creating and maintaining the sense of such needs.[56] In the end, risk society and consumer society combine forces in a self-perpetuating cycle of risk and counter-risk that sustains and stimulates New Age capitalism.

Aromatherapy and Gendered Identities

That women are the primary targets for and consumers of aromatherapy products cannot be surprising. Women have long been linked with perfume and fragrance, with flowers and nature, with cosmetics and beauty. Aromatherapists may be hoping to enlarge their consumer base by emphasizing the ancient use of aromatics by members of both sexes, but for now aromatherapy sales are primarily sustained by women. The percentage of female consumers varies from one company to another as well as from one type of company to another. In general, the higher end, independent essential oil suppliers tend to have a slightly more mixed clientele because many of the oils are purchased for medicinal and therapeutic purposes. The president of one of these suppliers, Aroma Therapeutics, estimates that about 70 percent of the company's customers are women.[57] In the more mainstream retail outlets like Bath & Body Works, essentially all of the customers are women. It seems the closer aromatherapy is to practice, the more sex-balanced the consumer base, a correlation which highlights the fact that when aromatherapy practices are transformed into products they carry with them ideologies of gender.

The discourse surrounding aromatherapy sounds a lot like the rhetoric of women's magazines—a *Cosmo* type of take-charge pseudo-feminism—which suggests that women can control everything from their weight to their romance and thus live perfectly contented lives. Women's magazines are probably the quintessential means of perpetuating hegemonies of beauty, upholding socially sanctioned ideals of what a body should look like, and generally pushing women to subscribe to damaging ideologies of themselves. Thus, the similarity between the rhetoric of women's magazines and the rhetoric of aromatherapy is a potent one. Despite its New Age and earth-friendly associations, aromatherapy fosters similar ideas, suggesting that women can attain cosmetic and spiritual perfection by taking responsibility for their beauty and well-being through the use of the proper products.

A survey of women's magazines published before and after the 1970s feminist movement reveals the longevity and power of these messages in the construction of women's lives.[58] In the late 1950s, women's magazines were full of articles like "Hair Do's and Don't's," "Prettier Hair: Ten Problems and How to Handle Them," "The Magic of Make-up," and "*Redbook*'s Beauty Quiz," all suggesting that women could maximize their beauty potential by following the magazines' directions. In the late 1980s, women's magazines were full of the same articles, though coded in a slightly more "feminist"-sounding rhetoric. The "Hair Do's and Don't's" and "The Magic of Make-up" became "Everything you always wanted to know about beauty and fashion" but still offered directions for hair care and styling, make-up application, and body-toning. Again, the message is clear: a woman's potential (for beauty, for being a woman, for happiness) is not only hers to control but also her responsibility. With aromatherapy, the ideology of women's magazines is simply reinscribed onto product packaging and into product catalogues. Again, women are encouraged to fulfill their beauty potential by working through their bodies, part by part. Thus, the aforementioned skin care products for the face, the aromatherapy treatments for cellulite, the essential oil shampoos for shinier, healthier, stronger hair all push women into the modes of consumption required to sustain New Age capitalism.

Such ideologies of beauty, health, and happiness also work in conjunction with the popular belief that a woman's fulfillment derives from her relationships with others, particularly men. One of the driving forces behind women's magazines, this idea also contributes to the overall tenor of aromatherapy discourse. Beauty and health are conflated with sexuality and romance, and virtually every line of aromatherapy products includes a fragrance or a blend that captures this nexus of beauty, health, sexuality, and romance—A Little Romance (Bath & Body Works), Sensuality (Coty), Sensuous (Smith and Vandiver in J. C. Penney stores), and Gabriel Blend (Archangel Essence), a blend that "mixes sandalwood and sweet orange blossom for a sensual aroma that creates a romantic feeling."[59] As with all of these scents and blends, Bath & Body Works' A Little Romance not only sets the proper mood for inspiring romance but also exfoliates, moisturizes, and softens skin, depending on the specific version of the product. Aromatherapy sells more than essential oils and the promise of holistic health. Aromatherapy also sells the dominant ideologies of beauty and romance, and it is these gendered ideals that in turn compel women to the market.

It is also these ideologies—together with an increasing number of environmental illnesses and multiple chemical sensitivities—that have motivated anti-fragrance movements in a variety of places throughout the country and particularly among more activist women's and lesbian communities. One of the most widely known scent-free policies was introduced by the School of Social Work at the University of Minnesota in 1993. The policy, which applies only to Ford Hall where the School of Social Work is located, is not a law but more of a request with some power behind it: "Please refrain from wearing scented personal care products when spending time in Ford Hall. This request is made to accommodate those disabled by environmental illness. Persons who wear scented products in classrooms and other relatively small enclosures will be asked to leave if there are persons with allergies in the area."[60] Students in Ford Hall have been asked to leave classes to wash off scented lotions and perfumes before returning. Though some students see the antifragrance policy as an extension of the political correctness movement, a sign of intolerance, and an infringement of individual rights, most take it seriously as a result of a severe reaction one woman suffered in response to a fragrance.[61]

Like the University of Minnesota School of Social Work's request, most policies are just that, policies and not laws. However, advocates for fragrance-free workplaces and public spaces contend that laws may be permissible under the 1990 Americans with Disabilities Act, a federal statute that requires employers to accommodate workers with disabilities, and many are researching the legislative prospects.[62] A similar policy exists with the San Francisco Board of Supervisors, and other Bay Area cities like Marin and Berkeley are trying to pass similar policies.[63] The San Francisco policy asks that people who attend the board meetings accommodate those with multiple chemical sensitivity, and a request to this effect is printed on all agendas for upcoming meetings. While no one is barred from the meetings as a result of too much fragrance, employees do have the right to ask heavily scented individuals to move further away.[64]

The San Francisco Board of Supervisors' policy gives institutional backing to a long-standing trend among women's activist organizations in the San Francisco Bay Area. At the Women's Building, a four-story structure that houses eight women's organizations and provides low-cost rental space for a variety of community events and group meetings, most events are advertised as "scent free please" out of consideration for the unusually large number of women who have allergies to scented products. One woman, Laura X, who runs a clearinghouse for information on date rape out of her home in Berkeley, requests that all visitors shower at her home, using the scent-free products that she supplies, before meeting with her and entering the clearinghouse. In general, the dominant cultural practice among women in these communities is to go as scent-free as possible at all times.

Clearly, for many women, the movement against scented products stems from serious medical conditions like multiple chemical sensitivity.[65] However, for many other women, the cause seems a healthy way of resisting not only scented products but also the more general discourses of commodity culture with their attendant ideologies of gender. For many women, the two are simply flip sides of the same coin. For instance, Amy Unger-Weiss, a woman with multiple chemical sensitivity and one of the University of Minnesota students responsible for establishing the School of Social Work's scent-free policy, resists the ideology of perfume advertisements while advocating for easy breathing: "When Unger-Weiss thinks about perfumes—be they expensive imports or dime-store eye-burners—she doesn't think of sweet odors and romance. She thinks of toxic molecules evaporating from the body of one person and being breathed in by an innocent bystander."[66] From this perspective, scent quickly goes from the mass-marketed "sweet odors and romance" to the debilitating "toxic molecules."

Of course, women are not the only ones to suffer from too much scent. Many men also express interest in creating fragrance-free workplaces. There seems to be one fundamental difference between women's and men's desire for scent-free spaces. Whereas women tend to advocate for scent-free policies because of environmental illnesses and their desire to resist the ideologies associated with fragrances, most men tend to support such policies because they find strong fragrances annoying. For instance, Dan O'Brian, president of Oswald Risk Management Services, says of one woman's perfume: "It could have killed a horse at 25 feet." One man who works in an accounting firm even stops breathing while riding the elevator with some of the more heavily perfumed women in his building. Professional women respond in kind; one described an elevator full of men wearing Obsession as "an upscale monkey house at the zoo."[67] For the most part, however, complaints about aggressive perfumes are issued by men about women, at least partially due to the fact that women tend to wear perfume and scented products much more frequently than men do.

However, these complaints might also represent protest and resistance on men's part, though not necessarily resistance to the market-driven ideologies of beauty. Rather, it seems possible that in speaking out against fragrances—and particularly perfumes—in the workplace, men are also speaking out against women in the workplace. Though some men use scented aftershaves and colognes, perfumes are overwhelmingly associated with women, and the resistance to perfume may be a coded protest against women in the workplace. Such a possibility lends insight into some men's particularly harsh complaints about various perfumes, like the one that "could have killed a horse at 25 feet." If perfumes represent women, then the more aggressive ones are the more threatening ones. Rather than suffer the potentially horse-killing scent with which this one prospective client had perfumed herself, Dan O'Brian used a little white lie to move the meeting to a larger room with the hopes that the extra space would dilute the smell somewhat. After all, as he says, "It was a matter of survival."[68] Here, his business survival depends on getting rid of her perfume.

It makes little difference to the market whether scented products or unscented products are used more frequently. Even the most idealistic portrayal of the anti-fragrance movement as resistance to consumer culture and its attendant ideologies of gender, health, and beauty is absorbed by capitalist innovation which simply sells consumers their own message of resistance with their new, scent-free products. A number of mass-produced everyday pro-ducts—shampoos and conditioners, floor cleaners and dish detergents, laundry soaps and underarm deodorants—have all been available in scent-free varieties for several years.

Headquartered in Minnesota, Aveda began working with the Chemical Injury Resource Association (also of Minneapolis) after learning of multiple chemical sensitivity from the publicity surrounding the University of Minnesota School of Social Work scent-free policy. According to Aveda's own publicity, learning about multiple chemical sensitivity provided Aveda the opportunity to further expand on the company's commitment to people with sensitive skin by developing a product line that could be tolerated by those with severe sensitivity. After years of research and development, Aveda found that most people with multiple chemical sensitivity can tolerate natural ingredients if they are food-grade (meaning pure enough to eat). Aveda's All-Sensitive product line was born. Other aromatherapy, cosmetics, and bath and body companies have followed suit. Even local independent retailers like Body Time in Berkeley offer many of their products unscented, though probably not pure enough to eat: "A great number of our products have no scent or color added . . . a benefit to those with allergies or sensitive skin."

In the true spirit of capitalist innovation, scent-free products serve two purposes. On the one hand, scent-free products are available for those with multiple chemical sensitivity or for those who opt to bypass the traditional associations that fragrances imply. On the other hand, they open up the possibility of an entirely new market—people interested in custom-scenting everything from shampoos and hair gels to lotions and body oils. Thus, two new markets emerge from a social movement that posed a potential threat to businesses predicated on smells and fragrances.

The Aveda Corporation

Because of its size, international reputation, and marketing acumen, Aveda and its "lifestyle magazine" provide an excellent opportunity for a more detailed look at the ideologies at work when aromatherapy practices are transformed into commodities for a market economy. Aveda's founder, Horst Rechelbacher, introduced the notion of aromatherapy to the American public in the mid-1970s when he started Aveda with a few batches of "pure plant shampoo" he had whipped up in his kitchen. Since then, he has introduced a diverse variety of products "imbued with the multiple benefits of pure flower and plant ingredients," including hair and skin care products, a full line of hair and skin care products for individuals with multiple chemical sensitivity, cosmetics, personal fragrances and "purefumes," aromatherapy paraphernalia for the home, even home cleaning products and nutritional supplements. According to the company's website and lifestyle magazine, the Aveda philosophy is premised on "environmentally responsible business practices and lifestyles," and Rechelbacher is as well known for being an "international leader in corporate activism, environmental standards and ground breaking products" as he is for founding Aveda.[69]

The Aveda philosophy sounds like a treatise in response to the hazards of risk society. The company's mission statement delineates the ways in which Aveda—through the production of aromatherapy and other plant-derived products—takes a moral stance with respect to the earth's resources. Aveda is emblematic of the New Age corporation. According to its lifestyle magazine, not only does Aveda search "the globe for wild-harvested plants or those grown without the use of petrochemical fertilizers, insecticides, or herbicides," but the company also offers an alternative to the use of petrochemicals which pollute "our soil, water, air, and bodies." In addition, the company prides itself on making intelligent use of the planet's resources, supporting the rights of indigenous peoples, and not conducting animal testing. Of course, through the use of products, the reader-consumer is encouraged to participate in these environmentally sound programs to help ensure that the ills of modernity do not destroy "the future of our species": "In the end, issues of environmental and social responsibility will determine the future of our species. At Aveda, we believe that tomorrow will arrive through the use of renewable resources, sustainable development, and constructive environmental practices. . . . But the real key to our success, of course, lies in our products. Unmatched in quality and effectiveness, they do what they claim to do. And they do it in such a pleasing manner that you'll want to keep on using them, which is the whole idea."

In his introduction to the magazine, Rechelbacher articulates these themes and makes more explicit the ways in which personal and planetary care are entwined:

> In today's world, it's easy to lose sight of one's interconnection with nature. This magazine exists to reveal those connections, to strengthen our awareness of cause and effect on a personal level—and to offer positive choices for living life in balance with ourselves and the Earth . . .
>
> At Aveda, we consider ourselves a biological organization, and our mission is to bring about positive effects through responsible business methods. We do this, quite frankly, out of self-preservation. We want to sustain ourselves, and by so doing, demonstrate that one's life and one's business can be conducted in a way that respects all cultures, all creatures, all the wisdom on the face of the Earth.

Here, Rechelbacher touches on many of the themes commonly invoked in the discourse surrounding aromatherapy, particularly that of environmental responsibility. Rechelbacher presents the lifestyle symbolized by the individual use of aromatherapy products as a feasible way of countering the poisons of techno-industrial society. Moreover, he situates aromatherapy, and specifically Aveda products, at the center of an alternative lifestyle that brings together environmental concerns, a feel-good multiculturalism, a platform of animal rights, and ultimately self-preservation.

Both the company's mission statement and Rechelbacher's introduction set the agenda for the remaining eighty-five pages of the Aveda Lifestyle magazine. All of the articles and photographs elaborate the various themes introduced in the opening few pages, creating a slick "educational" advertisement that teaches reader-consumers how to use Aveda products for better health and for a better world.

The magazine proper opens with a showcase article about Aveda's business "partnership" with the Yawanawa people who live "deep in the rainforest of western Brazil." Aveda's depiction of the primary Yawanawa village, Nova Esperanca, distinguishes the Yawanawa's living conditions and lifestyle from those of the magazine's readers and Aveda's consumers: "A cluster of wooden, thatched-roof huts, loosely arranged around a central clearing, forms the heart of the village. There, the conveniences the rest of the world takes for granted do not exist: there is no plumbing, no electricity, and the nearest town for purchasing goods is a few days' trip downriver when the water is high enough for travel. Most food is grown, gathered, raised, or hunted, and drinking water comes from nearby streams. The tribe's only way of communicating with the outside world: a two-way radio that runs off a car battery recharged by one small solar plate." Complementing the article's opening paragraphs describing the lengthy and treacherous trek through the rainforests to Nova Esperanca, this sketch of the village authenticates the indigeneity of the Yawanawa by creating an effect of temporal and spatial distance from the reader. Distancing the Yawanawa in time and space is an act of romantic colonization: on the one hand, the Yawanawa are presented as still living in accordance with nature, their "interconnection with nature" as yet unbroken; on the other hand, such a celebration of the Yawanawa confines them to stereotyped, iconic categories of ethnic difference.[70]

After establishing that the Yawanawa are an indigenous people who live in remote Nova Esperanca, the Aveda magazine article delves into the history of the Aveda-Yawanawa business collaboration. As the story goes, Rechelbacher was in Rio de Janeiro for the Earth Parliament in 1992 when he noticed the way "the indigenous peoples in attendance used the [uruku] pigment for coloring their skin, craftwork, and fabrics." Rechelbacher and May Waddington, one of the local Earth Parliament organizers, met with sixteen tribes to discuss partnership possibilities for harvesting uruku pigment (to be used in Aveda lipsticks) and eventually decided to work with Biraci Brasil, chief of the Yawanawa tribe.

As it turns out, Biraci Brasil and the Yawanawa aren't the indigenous peoples of old anthropological monographs. In fact, the article highlights the chief's Western dress and compares him to a typical resident of Miami or Los Angeles. The chief is interested in much more than his "bright colored T-shirts, rubber flip-flops, and fierce games of pick-up volleyball," however; "Most striking about Bira is his powerful sense of spirituality and purpose, and his profound awareness of the challenges facing his tribe. Foremost among these is reclaiming the Yawanawa culture, which was nearly erased by decades of domination by rubber barons and missionaries." Embedded in the contrast between Chief Biraci Brasil's Western dress and his "sense of spirituality and purpose" is the implication that the typical residents of Miami or Los Angeles or any similar city lack this spirituality and purpose, a common critique of modernity. Though he may look modern, Chief Biraci Brasil and the Yawanawa still represent the unspoiled and romantic peoples of "the rainforest" and other similarly dangerous (yet somehow pure) locales.

Aveda presents itself in contrast to the rubber barons and missionaries, though ironically the missionaries believed that they were "helping" the Yawanawa, just as Aveda does. Aveda provided the money for planting 13,000 uruku seedlings as well as for "modern day intrusions" like a seed removal machine and another machine for grinding and blending the uruku. The article also notes, in a parenthetical aside, that the machines run on diesel fuel, though the tribe is exploring the use of "ecologically sound solar power." Chief Biraci Brasil imagines the tribe as a business of sorts, and everyone works to tend and harvest the uruku. Through economic self-sufficiency, the

Yawanawa hope to become completely independent of missionary influences (now a divisive factor within the tribe) and to stave off foreign influences like "outsiders who still want the land for their own economic gain." Aveda presents itself without irony as the means by which the Yawanawa can attain this independence and maintain their cultural traditions: "The Yawanawa are now better able to resist this interference because of the economic independence they have achieved through their partnership with Aveda."

In similar fashion, Aveda is also exploring possible collaborations with the Caiuá, Guarani, and Terena peoples to harvest plants for pigments and nutritional uses. Twenty years after they were "convinced . . . to cut down their noble woods with the promise that all would receive a house in return," the three tribes are living on a reservation in central Brazil because the deforestation has left them with "nothing: no birds, no game, no wood for burning or building, and no houses." The case of the Caiuá, the Guarani, and the Terena has become a "cause célèbre in Brazil," and Aveda says it hopes to rectify the damage by introducing partnerships like the one it has established with the Yawanawa.

From this elaborate collaboration with the Yawanawa, Aveda produces the pigments for only four of its approximately thirty-five lipstick colors. Uruku is a natural pigment, varying in color from harvest to harvest, which means more work at the Aveda laboratories to maintain consistency of color for their customers. However, as should be clear after reading the article, the extra effort and the long process are worth the benefits to the Yawanawa, to the rainforest, and to the environment in general. If that's not convincing enough, Aveda also points out that the extra effort (and extra cost) of uruku-based lipsticks offer health benefits to the user: "Considering the amount of lipstick you eat off your lips during the day, a year, a lifetime, we think you'll agree."

Again, social responsibility and personal health combine for effective advertising of aromatherapy products and cosmetics. In fact, given the current consumer trends in favor of environmentally friendly natural cosmetics and fragrances, Aveda's investment of 13,000 uruku seedlings and two machines seems like a pittance when compared to the return in terms of the company's image, marketing, and sales.

The Aveda-Yawanawa business collaboration is only one of the company's environmentally motivated endeavors. The Aveda lifestyle magazine itself is printed with "vegetable ink on processed elementally chlorine-free paper with 10% post-consumer waste," and the company requests that readers recycle it or pass it on to a friend when finished with it. Other efforts include a vast array of products that invoke this eco-consciousness in the product names themselves: Air-o-Sol spray, Pure-Fume scents, Intelligent Nutrients vitamins. For instance, Air-o-Sol hairspray offers an air-powered system for dispensing hairspray to avoid using an aerosol pump, which contributes to depletion of the ozone layer through the release of non-renewable hydrocarbon propellants. All products are sold in recyclable containers with as little excess packaging and labeling as possible. Through these measures and the company's intensive advertising emphasizing its sensitivity to ecological concerns, Aveda has developed a system which is good for the planet, good for the body, and good for the company's bottom line.

Rechelbacher's desire to help consumers reestablish and/or maintain their "interconnection with nature" extends beyond Aveda's environmentalism. Rather, the theme summarizes the company's extensive and creative use of the logic and assumptions of risk society. The Aveda lifestyle magazine presents a range of common personal and planetary risks associated with modernity—environmental destruction, bodily and emotional stress, the toxic effects of synthetic products in cosmetics, foods, medicines, cleaning products, and the environment—and then "educates" the reader-consumer as to how Aveda products and institutions can help counter these threats.

In general, Rechelbacher and Aveda foreground the importance of returning to "ancient" traditions and belief systems as the primary means of counteracting the destructive forces of modern life. For instance, the Aveda magazine upholds the five-thousand-year-old Indian system of Ayurvedic medicine as a way of achieving "balance" in the midst of "today's fast-paced world," a world that doesn't permit us to control "our bosses, the weather, crime, or the stock market." However, as Aveda points out, this crazy world does allow us to determine how we respond to these uncontrollable factors in our lives and thus enables us to attain "balance": "In practical terms, 'balance' translates into less stress, greater mental and physical vitality, and a more focused, contented state of being. To achieve it, more people are turning to age-old philosophies, signaling a new modern paradigm for self-care. . . . To Ayurvedic doctors, balance is no accident. They believe in a profound mind-body link in which the human body's inherent intelligence creates impulses that direct it to the right choices for well-being." To help foster this type of perfect balance, Aveda created the Personal Blends line of custom-scented hair and skin care products based on the ancient Indian science of Ayurveda. Here, in a move similar to that connecting aromatherapy to the ancient use of aromatics, Rechelbacher reduces the complex system of Ayurvedic medicine to the aspects of it that refer to the use of essential oils. Ayurveda becomes aromatherapy, which becomes Aveda.

Of course, achieving a balanced life requires more than just Ayurvedic medicine; the process also requires a "new technology that helps demonstrate the efficacy of aroma on emotional states: bioactivity cameras." Thus, the exotic philosophy of Ayurvedic medicine is realized through modern biotechnology in a tension that recalls the romantic colonization of the Yawanawa. We need ancient therapies as modernity threatens to destroy us through its successes; nevertheless, we require modern technologies to best reproduce the benefits of ancient philosophies in a commercial setting. Customers are encouraged to undertake a "Sensory Journey" at an Aveda retail location to find the aromas that will restore them to balance: "You experience aromas, without labels or suggestion, until you find those that evoke an 'ahh' response. This gut reaction is a direct link to your senses—the 'deepest self' that responds to what you need for balance and nurturing *at that time*" (my emphasis). Here, the philosophy of aromatherapy practices is thoroughly commodified as Aveda creates a system for ensuring a perpetual consumption of products. The "deepest self" may know what scents are necessary for balancing and nurturing "at that time," but the (not surprising) fact that such needs change also means that the "deepest self" must choose a variety of scents for all of the other times when it needs balancing.

Aveda relies on the virtual impossibility of this task to keep customers filing into the company's stores, salons, and spas for Sensory Journeys and custom-scented products. The permutations of Personal Blends products are seemingly infinite: a range of scents determined by the whims of the "deepest self" can be combined with a range of products including "pure-fume" (natural perfume), oils for diffusers, cleansers, moisturizers, massage products, shampoos, conditioners, even professional hair treatments like perms and colors. Aveda's endless Personal Blends sales plan further evokes a self-indulgent attitude toward health and wellness: "'This is self-nurturing and caring on a very deep level,' says Horst Rechelbacher. 'With Aveda Personal Blends, you can make every moment your best moment—by identifying the aromas that help you relieve tension, stress, or depression, and using them for total personal care.'" In essence, seeking balance and resisting the ills of modernity is a costly endeavor, but again, personal health and well-being are worth the sacrifice.

For the somewhat less indulgent (or less "responsible"), Aveda has another line of products based on the ancient science of Ayurveda. The Chakra aromas are premixed scents based on the Ayurvedic principle of the seven chakras or centers of energy in the body. Aveda has reinterpreted the seven Chakras by giving them names to help the consumer determine which Chakra aroma is best suited for the moment or mood: Chakra I: Motivation, Chakra II: Attraction, Chakra III: Equipoise, Chakra IV: Fulfillment, Chakra V: Creative, Chakra VI: Intuition, and Chakra VII: Bliss. Here, the Aveda names are much more enticing than the traditional ones: base, hara (located in the lower intestine), stomach, heart, throat, mid-brain, and crown.[71] Implicit in this semantic transfer is also an ideological transfer, a move from the realm of the physical to the realm of the psychological. Anatomy and physiology—base, stomach, heart, mid-brain—quickly become singular purposes and static states of being—motivation, fulfillment, intuition. Typical of the discourse of commodified bodily practice, such a semantic transfer contains the dynamic and expansive possibilities of the chakras as they exist in Ayurvedic medicine, thus making an "exotic" system of practice easily accessible for consumption. Not only are individual chakras capable of influencing a range of outcomes, both physical and emotional, they are also capable of working together with other chakras in a holistic system that is completely reduced when rendered as a product for the body.

Consumers can purchase the Chakra aromas as blends of essential oils or in a variety of products, and one need not rely on the whims of the "deepest self" for choosing the appropriate aroma since the names themselves can direct the buyer. In drawing on the Ayurvedic principle of the chakras, Aveda invokes the association with ancient practices and beliefs while also suggesting a fragrant and easy path to enlightenment and bliss, a shortcut bypassing the more traditional means of attaining these states of being through a difficult lifelong practice that includes yoga and meditation.

To sell the full range of its products and services, Aveda markets a holistic lifestyle, an attractive alternative to living with the ills of techno-industrial society. The Aveda Lifestyle magazine positions each product line within the more extensive structure and rhetoric of risk society and New Age capitalism by highlighting its eco-friendliness or its roots in ancient health systems or its acceptability to people with multiple chemical sensitivity. In so doing, Aveda continues to enhance the company's image as an antidote to the ills of modernity while also "educating" the reader-consumers as to the personal and ecological importance of integrating Aveda products into their lives.

Futhermore, the sheer number of products and services discussed in the Aveda lifestyle magazine can be somewhat daunting. Because each article makes every product line seem essential to good health and social responsibility, by the time one has finished the magazine it is difficult to imagine how to incorporate all of the products into daily practice. The reader-consumer is left with a clear sense that such a task is both possible and necessary, however. Aveda helps the reader-consumer manage the different products in the final article, entitled "Daily Rituals." Again, the themes of balance and interconnectedness with nature underpin the suggested Aveda Rejuvenating Rituals: "We need to regain a sense of balance in our lives with daily rituals that promote calm and well-being, and reinforce our appreciation of nature and our close connection to the natural world. Aveda Rejuvenating Rituals are pleasurable techniques that help restore balance to the mind, body, and spirit. . . . Enjoy them as a part of a healthful, nurturing approach to living." The word "ritual" itself imbues the commodification of aromatherapy—and the suggested uses for Aveda products in particular—with a certain spirituality. And, as many critiques of modernity make clear, contemporary life's lack of spirituality is responsible for many social evils. Here, Aveda benefits from popular attempts to claim—and revive—cross-cultural rituals for modern society, rituals which constitute the heart of the New Age movement.[72]

The word "ritual" also refers to daily habits, and thus the Aveda

Rejuvenating Rituals are presented simply as good daily practices. The list of daily rituals is comprehensive both in terms of ritual and in terms of Aveda products used to enhance the ritual experiences:

Wake-Up Incentives—Sensory Testing to determine the best Personal Blends essences for diffusing, misting, and using on pulse points to wake up.

A Workout for Body and Senses—energizing and relaxing massage oils for warming up and cooling down muscles before and after exercise.

Complete Care—hair care, skin care, and body care products for shower and bath; similar to those recommended here are the eight skin care products recommended for daily use in another article titled "Daily Regimen."

Smooth Shave—Aveda Shave Emollient, facial toner, Singular Note Purifying Water, After-Shave Balm, and soothing lotions customized with any Balancing Infusion.

Make an Appearance—a wide range of eco-conscious eye, cheek, and lip colors.

Earth Carewear—eco-conscious clothing from the Aveda Anatomy catalogue.

Mind Over Matter—aromas to assist with "meditation and contemplation" exercises as well as Aveda's invigorating Breath Elixir for an immediate "lift."

Nourished by Nature—Aveda's Intelligent Nutrients herbal dietary supplements.

Come Clean—Aveda Vital Elements household cleaners (fabric, dish, and all-purpose detergents) to avoid the use of petrochemical based detergents and cleaners.

Air Lift—Aveda Aroma Mists, Aroma Diffusers, Essential Oils, and Plant Pure-Fume Aroma Candles.

Scents of Balance—Stress-Relieving Treatments and blends with names like Amour, Chi, and Relax.

Pure Knowledge—Aveda Lifestyle Workshops, Aveda Institute courses, and Aveda Spa seminars.

Incorporating all of these rituals into a single day would leave little time for anything else. Aside from that, the full descriptions of each ritual make explicit the way that each specific ritual will help the individual take responsibility for herself, her health, her body, her beauty, her emotions, and the environment. For instance, the entry for Air Lift advises: "Whenever you seek to create a pleasant, balancing personal atmosphere—on your body, clothes, and linens, or in the house, office, or car—opt for the true scents of nature. Real flower and plant aromas have the natural ability to soothe the mind and the senses—something no synthetic-based perfume or air freshener can duplicate." Here, personal balance and personal environment are interwoven with nature, and the boundaries between the two are blurred as office, house, and car take on the fragrances of flowers and plants.

Aveda's "Daily Rituals" brings the Aveda Lifestyle magazine full circle with a practical rearticulation of the opening mission statement and letter from Horst Rechelbacher. Aveda's complete and thorough commodification of aromatherapy creates a forum in which the company can unite and capitalize on ideologies of beauty, health, and spirituality with the rhetoric of risk society while simultaneously positioning itself as the antidote to the destructive advances of techno-industrial, modern societies.

Conclusion

Aveda's commodification of aromatherapy may be an extreme case, but it is also a telling case. With Environmental Lifestyle Stores throughout the world, Aveda attests to the growing popularity of aromatherapy products. From the higher-end Aveda products to the mass-marketed products like those developed by Bath & Body Works,

J. C. Penney, and Coty, aromatherapy in its commodified form sits at the center of a complicated discourse, linking ideologies of gender, health, beauty, and sexuality with environmentalism, anti-modernity, the general health of the planet, and the sustainability of all of its living species. As aromatherapy is commodified and transformed from a practice into a series of products, consumers—particularly women—are encouraged to take greater responsibility for the personal, political, and planetary dangers of risk society.

3

MACROBIOTIC EATING

Like aromatherapy, macrobiotic eating advocates a holistic approach to health and wellness. But where smelling certain scents may be healing, relaxing, pampering, and pleasurable, eating is—in addition to these things—essential to life itself. Thus macrobiotic eating is presented as a holistic approach to living. The commodification of macrobiotic eating is more nuanced than is the commodification of aromatherapy; nonetheless, cooking utensils, food ingredients, prepackaged foods, restaurants, books, television shows, videos, and instructional courses are all available to help one live according to the tenets of the macrobiotic philosophy.

Through macrobiotic eating as a commodified version of cultural eating practices, contemporary American concerns about food, eating, and health intersect with ideologies of modernity, alterity, and environmentalism. At the same time, the reification of macrobiotic eating also fragments the mind and body, further entrenches a mechanized model of the body, and advocates mental control to overcome bodily desires for various foods, thereby calling into question the philosophy of holistic living upon which it is based.

Contemporary Macrobiotics

Macrobiotic eating was first articulated as a specific approach to healthy living by Hippocrates, who used the word "macrobio" in his essay "Airs, Waters, and Places." In bringing together "macro," which means "great" or "large," with "bio," meaning "life," Hippocrates coined a word to describe those who enjoyed health and longevity. Other classical thinkers like Herodotus and Aristotle later used the term "macrobiotic" to refer to the diet and lifestyle of those who were healthy and long-lived.

In the late eighteenth century, Christophe W. Hufeland, a German physician and philosopher, revived the concept of macrobiotic eating in his popular book *Macrobiotics, or The Art of Prolonging Life*. It wasn't until the late nineteenth century, however, that the current macrobiotic movement began. Two Japanese educators, Sagen Ishitska, M.D., and Yukikazu Sakurazawa, cured themselves of "serious illnesses" by eating what has come to be the standard macrobiotic diet of brown rice, miso soup, sea vegetables, and other "traditional foods" (i.e., traditional Japanese foods). Yukikazu Sakurazawa emigrated to Paris in the 1920s, and he later renamed himself George Ohsawa.

Ohsawa is widely recognized as the founder of the modern macrobiotic movement; for him, macrobiotic eating was as much about health and longevity as it was about spirituality, love and freedom, and "absolute happiness." In fact, he believed that obstacles to understanding love and freedom as the same concept derived from physiological obstacles brought about by poor eating and drinking habits: "People cannot seem to understand that the principle of freedom and that of love are one and the same. It is ignorance of this principle that causes all the unhappiness and tragedies of this world. . . . This color blindness [of memory and reason] has a dominant influence on our spiritual and mental constitution, which is dependent upon our physiological constitution. Just as the function of a machine depends on its physical and mechanical construction, our mental and spiritual functions also depend greatly on our way of eating and drinking, which largely determine our physiological constitution."[1] This holistic approach to life—the integration of spirituality with physical health and wellness—is the cornerstone of the macrobiotic philosophy as defined and taught by Ohsawa. Ohsawa devoted his life to international proselytizing of macrobiotic eating: he delivered the macrobiotic message in more than thirty countries, gave more than 7,000 lectures, and published over three hundred books.[2]

Among Ohsawa's many disciples was Michio Kushi, now the world's leading authority on macrobiotic eating and the self-proclaimed "leader of the international macrobiotic community."[3] Kushi was born and raised in Japan, and (according to most sources) he graduated with a degree in international law from Tokyo University before coming to the United States to continue his graduate studies in 1949. While at Columbia University, Kushi began teaching macrobiotics and found it so rewarding that he decided to devote his life to it. An alternative and more recent scenario—also scripted by Kushi—rewrites this history, omitting Ohsawa's influence while also portraying his current interests in world peace as motivation for his life's devotion to the philosophy of macrobiotic living: "Kushi graduated from Tokyo University having studied philosophy and English literature. Upon witnessing the devastation of World War II, he de-cided to dedicate his life to the achievement of world peace and the development of humanity." This version of Kushi's biography suggests that he came to his own understanding of the principles of macrobiotic eating through his studies of "oriental philosophers who taught that food was the key to health and health the key to peace."[4] The differences in the versions of Kushi's biography are not crucial to an understanding of the philosophy of macrobiotic living, but they are interesting insofar as they reflect Kushi's own repackaging of himself and of macrobiotic eating over time.

Kushi brought macrobiotic eating to its current position of commodified glory. Early in his career as a macrobiotic teacher, he noticed that many of his students had difficulty locating the foods he recommended for the diet, so he started a natural foods business to meet the demand he was generating. His company, Erewhon, blossomed into a $17 million business by the mid-1980s and still produces natural foods today, though it no longer restricts itself to macrobiotic fare.[5] In 1994 Kushi developed another whole foods company called Kushi Macrobiotics Corporation, which oversees Kushi Natural Foods. Since its inception, it has grown into a $3 million company with annual sales for the 1997-1998 fiscal year around $700,000.[6] Kushi and his wife also founded the Kushi Institute and the East West Foundation, two nonprofit organizations de-voted to educating people about macrobiotic eating, as well as the One Peaceful World publishing house.[7] The Kushi Institute offers a broad range of courses for macrobiotic living as well as instruction for those interested in careers as macrobiotic counselors and cooks. The East West Foundation publishes books and a monthly magazine and initiates research into the benefits of macrobiotic eating.

Eating macrobiotically also requires various specific cooking utensils like salad presses, special knives, wooden bowls, pressure cookers, and *suribachis* (Japanese ridged bowls which function somewhat like a large mortar and pestle), all of which Kushi describes in his various books on macrobiotic living and which he makes available for purchase through the Kushi Institute website and catalogues. The macrobiotic way also strongly recommends that people remove any unnatural materials from their lives, including most toothpastes, many soaps and shampoos, and many textiles (including dyes); to help people find natural toothpastes, soaps, shampoos, detergents, clothing, towels, and linens, the Kushi Institute also sells many of these items through its catalogue. In addition, novelty items like aprons, One Peaceful World (the Kushis' publishing house and international organization for world peace through macrobiotic living) lapel pins, and teaching tools like videos are available.

In 1995, Kushi introduced a new line of natural foods called Kushi Cuisine. Kushi Cuisine is "a more convenient option based on many of the same [macrobiotic] principles" and it seeks to attract "crossover" consumers (also called "semi-vegetarians," "pseudo-vegetarians," and "transitional eaters")—people interested in eating vegetarian meals but not exclusively. Kushi Cuisine is a line of twenty-five natural foods—breakfast cereals, pasta and sauce combinations, rice and bean medleys, soups, condiments, and snacks—that require only five minutes to prepare.[8] Although the Kushi Cuisine products have no artificial ingredients, they are not necessarily macrobiotic.

The macrobiotic movement continues to expand, particularly in its commodified state. There are macrobiotic centers, consultants, and cooks throughout the United States and Canada, and the Kushi Institute has opened affiliate branches internationally. In Philadelphia, a macrobiotic chef who teaches cooking and lifestyle courses at the natural foods store Essene has just begun a series of public television shows which are taped at the store (and which will undoubtedly assist viewer-consumers in locating the necessary ingredients).[9] Macrobiotic living has even become a theme for vacations. MacroNews, the publisher of a Philadelphia-area macrobiotic cooking magazine of the same title, also offers "Macrobiotic Vacations to Exotic Destinations." The February 1998 vacation was to the Sandy Beach Island Resort in Barbados, where the trip's organizers promised to cook "delicious gourmet macrobiotic meals" while "you have fun making new friends, reacquainting with old friends, or just exploring all the treasures the island has to offer."[10]

Yin and Yang, Diet and Health: The Principles of Macrobiotic Living

The contemporary macrobiotic movement describes the macrobiotic lifestyle as a holistic approach to health premised on the belief that a "natural" diet is the single most important factor in helping a person achieve spiritual awakening and thus "genuine health": "Self-reflection leads us to abandon self-destructive habits and bring our way of eating and living into greater harmony with nature. A centrally balanced, macrobiotic diet based on whole cereal grains, beans, fresh local vegetables, and other whole natural foods is the most basic reflection of a way of life in harmony with nature. A naturally balanced diet provides the biological foundation for genuine health, while the spiritual foundation is provided by a deep sense of gratitude toward nature, the universe, and life itself." Living in harmony with nature is the central tenet of the macrobiotic diet because of the way in which "nature"—seasons, climates, environments—contributes to the yin or yang values of various foods, including the full range of consumable environmental matter like minerals, air, liquid, as well as "vibrations, waves, rays, and various forms of radiation." Two major principles of macrobiotic eating derive from this belief that we must live (and eat) in harmony with nature and the universal order: firstly, environmental matter must be consumed in a ratio which reflects the earth's current stage of planetary evolution, and secondly, the yin and yang values of foods must be balanced in conjunction with the natural environment.[11]

The proper ratio for the consumption of various foods and environmental matter is determined by the logarithmic spiral that characterizes the universe. Macrobiotic leaders Michio Kushi and Edward Esko contend that our universe takes the form of a gigantic logarithmic spiral with the ratio of one to seven.[12] Following this reasoning, one-to-seven ratios can be found throughout the natural world. Kushi and Esko offer the creation of the vegetable kingdom as an example: "The most recent vegetable species to appear were the cereal grains. Of these, there are five major types: rice, wheat, rye, millet, and barley. . . . Fruits are one step removed from cereal grains. Here there are thirty-five branches, or seven times five, each with many varieties. Leafy vegetables come next, and in this world, there are seven times thirty-five, or 245 major branches. The plant kingdom developed in the form of a logarithmic spiral, with cereal grains as the center, the end result."[13] Thus, to live in harmony with nature is to eat according to the one-to-seven ratio. Ideally, then, food should be eaten in one-to-seven ratios moving from mineral to protein, protein to carbohydrate, carbohydrate to water, water to air, and air to vibration. Kushi and Esko also use the one-to-seven ratio in the context of biological evolution as a way of further determining the proper macrobiotic dietary allotments. Thus, for instance, because humans have four canine teeth (for meat food) and twenty-eight incisors, premolars, and molars (for grains, beans, and vegetables), we should eat seven times (by weight) more vegetables than animal foods.

In addition, nutrients from land and sea vegetables should also be consumed as dietary supplements, even though they seem to fall outside of the predominant logarithmic spiral governing macrobiotic eating. Even when consuming these supplementary foods, however, Kushi and Esko recommend strict adherence to environmental order. For instance, while humans can eat anything which predated their existence on Earth, the philosophy of macrobiotic eating suggests choosing more vegetables from the more recent species and fewer from the ancient ones. Kushi and Esko provide a few practical guidelines to help illustrate the principle of maintaining order while selecting supplementary foods:

1. Soup should be a replica of the ancient ocean, and may consist of water, sea salt, enzymes, bacteria, sea vegetables, and/or occasional fish, land vegetables, beans, or grains.
2. Vegetable dishes should consist of a larger volume of modern species and a smaller volume of ancient species.
3. Fruits, nuts, and seeds may be used as supplements in small volume, due to their biological period which, in relation to other plant species, was comparatively short.[14]

Similarly, there are climatic, seasonal, and geographical orders to adhere to as well. Thus, people living in colder climates are advised to eat more animal foods, while people living in hot, semitropical climates should eat virtually no animal foods. In addition, cooking can also be used as a means of adapting foods to changes in temperature, humidity, and other climatic variations that accompany seasonal changes. For instance, in colder seasons, food should be cooked more thoroughly, while in warmer seasons it should be cooked less. Geographical restrictions vary depending on the food in question, but in general foods should be chosen from the nearest possible sources. Kushi and Esko recommend that air and water be taken from the immediate environment, while fruits should come from the same climatic and geographical area; vegetables, grains, and beans can be taken from a more extended geographical region (though similar to the immediate environment), and sea vegetables can be taken from the furthest extended area as long as it is in the same climatic belt.[15] According to these principles of macrobiotic eating, food should never be taken from the opposite hemisphere because of the extreme atmospheric, oceanic, and electromagnetic differences between the two hemispheres.

To eat in harmony with the universe also requires a thorough understanding of the yin and yang values of all foods. In ancient Chinese medicine and philosophy, yin and yang are the complementary energies found in all things. That is, everything contains both yin and yang energies, the only variations being the degree to which yin or yang energy predominates. Yin and yang correspond to the earth's force and heaven's force, respectively.[16] Along these lines, heaven's energy exerts a downward, contractive force and is thus yang, while the earth's rotation provides a centrifugal, upward force by which its energy is considered yin. The general characteristics of yin and yang provide a means of classifying foods according to their proper values: yin energy creates centrifugal force, expansion, diffusion, slowness, ascension, vertical growth, lightness, coldness, darkness, wetness, largeness, softness, gentleness, and a spiritual orientation; by contrast, yang energy creates centripetal force, contraction, fusion, assimilation, organization, fastness, horizontal growth, heaviness, hotness, brightness, dryness, thickness, hardness, activity, and material orientation.[17]

According to the macrobiotic philosophy of eating, food is classified by its yin and yang properties as a means of ensuring balance and harmony with nature and the universe. Different characteristics of the food—the climate where it grows, how quickly it grows, how much water it contains, where it grows with respect to the ground, and some of its dominant flavors—contribute to whether it is predominantly yin or predominantly yang. Because all foods (like all things) have both yin and yang qualities, the macrobiotic way relies on the food's growth cycle to help determine its energy value. For instance, during the colder fall and winter months, the "vegetal energy" and the atmospheric energy descend into the root system and the plant becomes more condensed. Thus, according to this reasoning, plant foods harvested in late autumn and winter—carrots, parsnips, turnips, cabbages—tend to be drier and more concentrated and thus more yang. During the warmer spring and summer months, energy is ascending as indicated by the new green leaves which appear as the weather warms. Plant foods harvested in the spring and summer months tend to contain more liquid, and those maturing late in the summer when the "vegetal energy has reached its zenith" are both juicy and sweet (like many fruits) and thus extremely yin.[18] And, just as the seasons influence the yin and yang qualities of various foods, so too do the geographical areas in which they are grown: hotter climates produce more yin foods while cooler climates produce more yang foods.

Due to the overall characteristics of plants and animals, foods from plant sources tend to be more yin while foods from animal sources tend to be more yang. For instance, vegetable species are grounded in one place, while animal species roam over large areas. Similarly, plants tend to grow in an expansive manner (branching outward and upward) while "animal bodies are formed in a more inward direction with compact organs and cells"; plants also tend to have cooler temperatures than animals, and plants convert carbon dioxide to oxygen whereas animals do the opposite.[19]

Characterizing foods according to the principles of yin and yang is an almost infinite process. Not only are foods classified in relation to other types of foods (foods from vegetable sources in relation to foods from animal sources, one type of vegetable in relation to another), but yin and yang values are also attributed to individual items of the same type of food. Thus, for instance, among apples, the smaller, harder, more bitter ones like crabapples are more yang than the larger, juicy ones like red Delicious; among crabapples, those which come from trees growing in sunny, stony environments are more yang than those growing on trees in soft soil and shady environments. Even crabapples from the same tree will differ in terms of yin and yang energy depending on factors such as the part of the tree on which they grow and the time of day at which they are picked.[20]

At the heart of the macrobiotic diet are the most balanced foods, those with relatively equal proportions of yin and yang energy—whole cereal grains, beans and bean products, root vegetables, leafy green vegetables, sea vegetables, spring and well water, non-stimulant teas and beverages, seeds and nuts, and temperate climate fruits.[21] Eating balanced foods is different from balancing yin foods and yang foods. In fact, macrobiotic eating seeks to overcome the predominant American tendency to balance one's diet by consuming foods from the extremes—meats, cheeses, eggs, and refined salt (extremely yang) coupled with frozen and canned foods, highly processed grains, tropical fruits, and ice cream (extremely yin). Advocates of macrobiotic eating highlight the body's natural tendency to attempt to balance yin and yang, a desire that causes a person to crave sweets, for example, after eating a meal of meats and other animal products. According to the macrobiotic way, it is difficult to balance a diet based on extreme yin and yang foods, and sickness often occurs as a result of excessive yin or yang energies.

Together, these two major principles—the one-to-seven ratio and the classification of foods into yin and yang—guide macrobiotic eating so that the individual remains in harmony with the natural environment and the universe. While it may seem virtually impossible to plan a meal given all of these considerations, macrobiotic teachers contend that following a macrobiotic diet for some time enables an intuitive understanding of these universal principles to emerge: "As we return to a condition of more sound physical and psychological health, we find that our bodies and minds intuitively respond to the environment according to these universal principles. The judgment according to yin and yang is nothing but the native, intuitive judgment of common sense."[22] Of course, prior to the point of intuitive understanding, advocates of macrobiotic living recommend cooking classes, macrobiotic lifestyle workshops, and if those are not available, cookbooks and videotapes.[23]

A macrobiotic diet is the key to eating in harmony with nature and the universe, but the macrobiotic philosophy is about more than just eating. For it to be most effective in generating holistic health, the macrobiotic approach must become a way of life. Suggestions for such a lifestyle are both practical and spiritual or philosophical. For instance, recommendations include chewing each mouthful of food at least fifty times (or until it becomes liquid), walking for approximately thirty minutes every day, scrubbing the body with a hot damp cloth rather than showering or bathing, and abstaining from wearing synthetic or woolen clothing next to the skin. Suggestions also advise against metallic accessories like rings, watches, bracelets, and necklaces (but if that is not possible, "keep such ornaments simple and graceful"; additionally, the suggestions say nothing about the "One Peaceful World" lapel pins sold through the Kushi Institute webpage), as well as avoiding perfumed cosmetics, electric cooking devices, and television. Suggestions for living more contented, fulfilling spiritual lives include living each day cheerfully, maintaining correspondence with all family members, teachers, and friends, keeping all personal relationships smooth and happy, and singing a song every day.[24] Proponents argue that such living, in conjunction with a macrobiotic diet, helps the "physical condition become cleaner and [the] memory clearer."[25]

Because of the logarithmic ratio of the universe, healing and spiritual well-being also occur at a one-to-seven ratio, such that one year of living according to the macrobiotic way changes both physical and mental conditions by seven years. According to Kushi and Esko, all physical and mental conditions reemerge as macrobiotic eaters move back along the spiral of time. Thus, to use their example, if someone beginning a macrobiotic regimen had pneumonia twenty-one years ago, he or she will reexperience it after three years of macrobiotic eating, though the symptoms will last for only a few days before spontaneously disappearing. After seven years of macrobiotic eating, people often experience difficulty with the diet because they have regressed along the spiral to an infantile state where they crave the foods of their infancy—mother's milk, which they translate into milk and sugar products. At the same time, however, seven years of macrobiotic eating also causes a person's perception to undergo substantial changes as he or she approaches infinity: "Purification of your embryonic period begins after seven years of macrobiotics. Your constitution also starts to heal. Your thinking changes. Your thoughts turn to your parents and then beyond. You remember the time when you were the foods your parents ate. Later, you regain memories of the animal and the vegetable world, and become aware of your kinship with these stages of life. You are able to see and understand the universe from their vantage point. Every level of life has a unique consciousness and you make contact with each as you retrace the steps of your origin to infinity." Through this new level of consciousness inspired by macrobiotic eating, a person understands the spirit of all things, thereby securing both physical health and spiritual contentment. The macrobiotic philosophy believes that as humanity evolves spiritually, universal vibrations will eventually replace food as we currently conceive of it and people will materialize out of the vibrations.[26] Until that time, however, macrobiotic eating offers a holistic approach to wellness while also guiding us toward this future of a highly spiritual humanity.

Romancing the Natural

Like aromatherapy, the philosophy of macrobiotic eating positions its history at both a spatial and a temporal distance from contemporary American culture. It thereby draws on the power of "ancient traditions" from remote cultures to lend it credence among those who equate dominant American (and/or Western, industrial, modern) culture with such ills as degenerative disease, obesity, environmental damage, materialism, and lack of spirituality. Most frequently, this spatial and temporal distancing emerges through contrasting descriptions of "traditional" diets and "modern" diets, the macrobiotic diet being among the "traditional" diets.

The modern diet is generally characterized by its excesses—too many refined and processed foods (specifically refined sugar), too many synthetic and artificial ingredients, too much saturated fat, too many animal products.[27] Moreover, in the modern diet these excesses take the place of "natural" foods, which provide necessary complex carbohydrates, fiber, vitamins, and minerals. By contrast, the traditional diet consists largely of whole grains, organic and locally grown fruits and vegetables, beans and bean products, and very limited quantities of animal foods.

Many of the macrobiotic representations of global eating practices place them in "way back" time, a time which was always present and is essentially undatable:

Throughout history, men have lived happy lives without complicated analytical concepts of nutrition.[28]
Thousands of years ago, here and there, some people attained universal consciousness and came to that conclusion [that food is important on physical, emotional, spiritual, and social levels].[29]
Macrobiotics is a way of eating and living that has been practiced *for thousands of years* by many people around the world.[30]
For countless generations, *since before the dawn of recorded history*, the majority of humanity ate a natural, ecologically balanced diet.[31]

Here, these descriptions recall a distant, romanticized past where food and eating were intuitively harmonious with nature. As Kushi and Esko point out, some people even "attained universal consciousness," which allowed them to articulate the more common, intuitive understanding of how balanced eating influenced physical, emotional, and spiritual health.

Most macrobiotic sources correlate the end of this intuitive ability to live and eat in harmony with nature and the universe with the agricultural revolution in the 1800s or with the Industrial Revolution. According to this thinking, the agricultural revolution resulted in an abundance of grains that made animal husbandry profitable, thus increasing supplies of meat and dairy products.[32] Those who blame the Industrial Revolution for altering the "traditional" diet also relate such shifts to an increase in disease: "A large-scale shift away from these traditional staples began with the Industrial Revolution and coincided with the rise of modern degenerative illnesses."[33]

Yet the movement away from these "traditional" diets of whole grains and local vegetables was under way long before the Industrial Revolution. As early as 3200 B.C.E., meat eating was a common practice in ancient Egypt, where livestock were bred, controlled, and ritually slaughtered. Meat eating was also an established practice in ancient Greece; cheese was a common feature of the daily meal, while meat was eaten during religious festivals, and even more frequently among the nobility who were wealthy enough to maintain their own herds.[34]

By the Renaissance, meat eating was the social norm in Europe and signified more than just gustatory choices: "Meat-eating had now become solidly entrenched in the mores of society. It was not only a matter of customs and manners, but was rooted deep in the psychology of behaviour backed by powerful sacral concepts." Menus from the Middle Ages highlight the extent to which meals centered on meat and animal products. One meal began with "brain in sharp sauce" and was followed by head of boar, young swans, capon, pheasant, heron, sturgeon, venison, suckling pigs, peacocks, cranes, rabbit, chickens, curlews, egrets, quails, snipe, and larks. Even "minor noblemen" enjoyed such hearty meals as beef, mutton, pork, veal, game and venison, carp, pike, eels, and lampreys. In general, feast meals such as these were structured around six courses—three meat courses followed by three fish courses. Each course ended with "a dish of pastry, a sweetmeat or a jelly," not exactly the whole grains, fresh vegetables, and legumes that characterize the "traditional" diet. In fact, such healthy fare was considered food for the poor and generally avoided by those who could afford "better." The poorest members of society did follow something of a "traditional" diet and survived on dairy products and whatever vegetables they could find growing locally, as well as on the foods given to them as compensation for their labor—pickled and smoked herring, whole grains like barley, wheat, and oatmeal—and beers and ales. While the peasant diet does seem to correspond loosely with the "traditional" or macrobiotic diet, most of these people tried to incorporate meat into their diets by poaching or, when especially desperate, by slaughtering their dairy animals. In any case, the poor who were essentially forced to live by this "traditional" diet were not intuitively drawn to it out of a sense of natural environmental harmony.[35]

Just as advocates of macrobiotic eating situate the "traditional" diet in a faraway past, they also distance it spatially by upholding small, relatively isolated cultural groups as exemplars of such traditional eating practices. For instance, several macrobiotic book authors refer to Dr. Alexander Leaf's survey of the dietary practices of various non-Western cultures with disproportionately high numbers (per capita) of centenarians.[36] Among the groups that Leaf visited were the Hunza of Kashmir and the Vilcabambans in the Ecuadorian Andes. He reported that the Hunza and the Vilcabamban diets were high in carbohydrates, with only moderate amounts of protein and fat and virtually no animal products. Essentially all of the proteins, oils, and fats were of vegetable origin, for the Hunza owing at least in part to the fact that the land is unsuitable for raising meat and dairy animals.[37] The environmental and social conditions that sustain the Hunza and Vilcabamban diets remain largely unexplored in these accounts, and thus it is difficult to determine the extent to which such dietary practices are motivated by an intuitive drive to harmonize with nature and the universe. Proponents of macrobiotics, however, continue to romanticize those who live by "traditional" diets: "As we have become somewhat removed from the natural elements, we have lost much that is valuable. We can learn a great deal from peoples such as the Hunzakuts, Vilcabambans, and the Abkhasians, who often live in continuous close contact with nature. They are vitally healthy and very active physically, many beyond their one-hundredth birthday."[38] Here, the macrobiotic discourse invokes a stereotypical connection between "exotic" peoples and "nature." In fact, the description of the Hunzakuts, the Vilcabambans, and the Abkhasians living in "continuous close contact with nature" recalls a similar characterization of the Yawanawa who harvest uruku in "partnership" with Aveda. As both the aromatherapy discourse and the macrobiotic discourse make clear, contemporary American culture would be much improved if only we could reestablish these connections with nature, connections that indigenous cultures supposedly understand and practice intuitively.

Not surprisingly, these macrobiotic book authors share only the parts of Leaf's findings that support a relationship between the macrobiotic diet and the diet of those who "live in continuous close contact with nature." A more complete and complicated picture emerges in Leaf's 1973 *National Geographic* article describing his research trip to Kashmir, to several different communities in the former Soviet Union, and to the Ecuadorian Andes. He begins by describing his visit with Khfaf Lasuria, a Georgian woman whose age is somewhere between 131 and 141: "I was greeted in warm Georgian fashion, and we toasted each other first with vodka and then with wine as we talked.... As she sat talking, she smoked cigarettes, inhaling each puff. She had started smoking in 1910, and has consumed about a pack a day for 62 years." The warm Georgian greeting doesn't recall any macrobiotic principles, except perhaps "living each day happily." While

Leaf does indeed speculate that a spare diet relatively high in carbohydrates and low in fat and protein—and meat and dairy products in particular—may prolong life and delay the onset of atherosclerosis, he also acknowledges the fact that the typical Georgian diet "muddles" his findings. Dairy products, meat, vegetables, and bread—a list containing three of the biggest "no-no's" on the macrobiotic diet—constitute the typical meal for about 60 percent of the Georgians over the age of eighty.[39] The same macrobiotic teachers who romanticize the Hunzakuts and the Vilcabambans fail to mention Khfaf Lasuria and any of the other Georgian centenarians in their representation of Leaf's findings.

The romanticization of the "natural"—and the macrobiotic diet as a means of living in harmony with nature—clearly plays a central role in the commodification of macrobiotic eating and the subsequent discourses surrounding it. In essence, the macrobiotic diet, the idea of improved health and fitness, the promise of a peaceful, stress-free lifestyle, and all the tools necessary to achieve these ideals are sold with the possibility of reestablishing such a connection to nature and the environment. The transformation of macrobiotic eating into a series of products enables and perpetuates the accompanying discourses through the proselytizing spirit of the diet's followers. In seeking to convert others to the macrobiotic way, the diet's proponents continue to foster this transformation through macrobiotic community centers, institutes, and restaurants, and through specialty foods (largely Japanese), natural foods, pre-packaged health foods, specialty kitchen utensils, natural dye-free textiles, and natural body care products.

Yet this proselytizing spirit is not necessarily motivated solely by a capitalist mentality (however much it might benefit from one). In fact, the desire to establish a greater connection with nature and the universe takes on an almost religious quality among adherents of the macrobiotic way. One macrobiotic cookbook attempts to introduce macrobiotic cooking while tempering this aspect of the movement: "It is the aim of the authors not to recommend and proselytize a mode of eating and living which requires monkish discipline, but rather to give instruction in the culinary road to a healthier life." At the same time, however, these authors still conceive of natural living as a religious or spiritual undertaking and a means of realizing an edenic past: "To live naturally is our only alternative in the world's mad rush towards total technology. We must never lose sight of the road back to Eden."[40] And, for those who do approach macrobiotic living with a religious zeal, macrobiotics provides a way of enacting some sort of "authentic" experience, an attempt to achieve a certain "purity" in a world perceived as impure, toxic, artificial, synthetic. Thus, Kushi and Esko see macrobiotics as a means of deliverance, a means of assisting the species as a whole to evolve to a higher level of existence, a "purer" level of existence: "Through macrobiotics, humanity can change direction and develop into a new species that is not bothered by the negative things that have been experienced in the past. Those who overcome and pass through the modern crisis can emerge as a new race with a new vision. . . . Modern intellectual humanity—*homo sapiens*—will evolve toward a new species, *homo spiritus*."[41] Thus, the romanticization of nature implicit in the commodified practice of macrobiotics attracts new followers who seek a means of opting out of the dominant American/Western culture of modernity. The consumption of a natural macrobiotic diet leads to an embodied "purity," a bodily statement and understanding of what it means to live out the ideology of the alternative.

Purity, Plain and Spiritual

The desire for pure food and pure living is presented as both practical and spiritual. On a practical level, the natural foods that contribute to the art of pure living combat the dangers of dining in a risk society—the threat of toxicity from environmental pollution, pesticides, and artificial ingredients. On a more spiritual level, such a lifestyle promises a certain connection with nature and an inner balance of body, mind, and soul, even a transcendence of worldly considerations. Making macrobiotic eating into a series of products and services positions the diet as a viable option for acquiring whatever type or degree of purity the consumer seeks at any given time, for any given period of time. That is, through the marketing of ideals as well as the commensurate products, the consumer has the power to choose macrobiotic eating for a lifetime, for a week-long retreat, for a meal, or even for a snack. In this way, the consumer also has the ability to trade in purities, to control the exchanges in the most beneficial manner, whether practical or spiritual, whether for planetary health or for personal wellness.

The practical desire for pure foods and the commodification of them based on their ability to combat toxicity and disease are not new trends. Among the most renowned nineteenth-century proponents of healthy living through food is John Harvey Kellogg, a doctor and Seventh-Day Adventist. Like Ohsawa, Kellogg's obsession with food and health developed after his own experiences with "serious childhood illnesses," experiences which led him to the work of Sylvester Graham, a health reformer who advocated a vegetarian diet as a means of avoiding gluttony which he saw as "the greatest of all causes of evil." Kellogg's work bears a striking similarity to Kushi's. In 1876 he converted the Western Health Reform Institute into the Battle Creek Sanitorium, a "university of health" where people could learn to stay well; like the Kushi Institute, it was frequented by celebrities and the wealthy of the day. Like Kushi, he also became a "stunningly successful entrepreneur in the business of improving health through food and lifestyle."[42] It is Kellogg's writings, however, that fully illustrate the similarity between issues of food and health at the turn of the century and today: "In consequence of our abuses and neglects, the human race is becoming dwarfed and weazened, neurotic, daft, dyspepsic, and degenerate . . . the perversions of our modern civilization . . . are responsible for the multitudinous maladies and degeneracies which yearly multiply in number and gravity."[43] Here, Kellogg's reference to "modern civilization" as the cause of both personal and social diseases recalls similar connections made throughout the macrobiotic discourse. And Kellogg was not alone in preaching the way to health through food and warning against the excesses of modernity. In 1885, Ellen Richards bemoaned the "use of improved methods of transportation" and "improved methods of preservation" because they fostered the dangers associated with an abundance of food from all over the world: "This very excess brings its own danger; for the appetite is no longer a sufficient guide to the selection of food, as it was in the case of the early people who were not tempted by so great a variety. Many diseases of modern civilization are doubtless due to errors of diet, which might easily be avoided."[44] Again, the themes of macrobiotic eating surface a century earlier—concern over eating too many foods from different parts of the world, concern over the loss of an inherent ability to recognize when the appetite is sated, concern over a possible connection between modernity and disease.

Michelle Stacey, a social historian of food and eating as well as a cultural critic, underscores the correlation between such beliefs in diet as medicine and fin-de-siècle attitudes about mortality, decay, purity, and rejuvenation: "This worldview—that we could control our fates through the science of health, and more specifically of eating—went on to reach two peaks. One was at the close of the nineteenth century; the other is at the close of [the twentieth] century."[45] As she points out, fin-de-siècle attitudes emphasize "anxieties about pollution and decay at century's end . . . desires for purification and rejuvenation at century's turn."[46]

This dual focus on pollution and purification captures the spirit of macrobiotic eating and permeates the rhetoric promoting the diet as a commodity. For instance, the Kushi Cuisine products center their image on this very duality, and their packaging all conveys the same message, on the box itself, "Michio Kushi, world-renowned father of the Standard Macrobiotic Diet, believes that with the right foods you can achieve harmony in Nature and Life. . . . Today, the Kitchens of Michio Kushi, under the watchful eye of Mr. Kushi himself, have created a small miracle . . . a family of prepared foods that actually taste good. In short, *perfect* replacements for *imperfect* foods" (emphasis in original). The banner across the front of all the Kushi Cuisine boxes uses the same line—"*perfect* replacements for *imperfect* foods"—as a subtitle under the Kushi Cuisine banner. Kushi Cuisine clearly positions its products as the "quick" and "easy-to-prepare" way to purify the body and soul of the imperfections of modern living and modern foods.

As with aromatherapy, the very act of commodification provides a forum for the macrobiotic discourse through packaging, advertising, and descriptions in catalogues. And, where aromatherapy offered an alternative to the medico-technological position on wellness and healing, macrobiotic eating offers a practical alternative to the foods contaminated by techno-industrial society at large. In both cases, the risk society discourse criticizes the successes of modernization that threaten to undermine our connections to nature and the bodily well-being that derives from such connections. Where food is concerned, two types of dangers arise through the successes of science characteristic of the risk society: on the one hand, there are environmental poisons (for example, side-effects like contaminated water, acid rain, and residual agricultural pesticides); on the other hand, there are suspicious laboratory creations intended to enhance the flavor of foods or to substitute for natural "dangers" like fat and sugar. Stacey describes the development of the contemporary natural foods movement as predicated on a fear of these two dan-gers: "That thinking [that food could be pleasurable] began to change again in the 1960s and 1970s, spurred this time by fear; the emerging environmental movement and the awareness of pesticides and preservatives that accompanied it made the words 'all natural' the most popular phrase on food labels. Health food stores began to prosper, as consumers became suspicious of food additives and more open to the notion of certain foods as health givers."[47]

Macrobiotic eating seems to anchor this natural foods movement; it is, in essence, the extreme end of the natural foods continuum. As should be clear from the macrobiotic tracts already cited, the diet reduces the risks of these hazards by shunning all artificial ingredients and preservatives, virtually all refined and processed foods (except those processed by "traditional" methods), vegetables grown with pesticides, and all animal foods (thus bypassing the potential danger of hormones). In preaching the extreme, macrobiotic teachers like Michio Kushi expand the boundaries of the health food movement and the health food market. Thus, relatively small health food companies like Kushi's own Erewhon could sustain themselves not only by meeting the needs of macrobiotic eaters but also by offering a "natural foods" option to more moderate health food eaters.

Ironically, the commodification of macrobiotic eating has also helped generate a more mainstream health foods movement best characterized as low-fat/no-fat, no/low-cholesterol, salt- and sugar-free. However, these low-fat/no-fat and sugar-free products tend to be highly processed and/or completely artificial, as in the cases of Simplesse fat substitutes for nonfat ice creams and NutraSweet sugar substitutes. The serialization of the "health food" category into these extremes—all natural macrobiotic foods on the one hand and synthetic fats, salts, and sugars on the other (and everything in between)—underscores the tensions between scientific "goods" and "bads" and the power of the market to exploit such tensions. While strict macrobiotics like the Kushis follow clear guidelines in choosing foods, others are likely to roam through the aisles of health food stores and supermarkets alike, the marketplace and the logic of New Age capitalism allowing them to define "health food" according to their individual desires and tastes.

Like the practical desire for pure foods, attempts to achieve spiritual purity through eating have a long history, in this case dating back further than Hippocrates and the first macrobiotic movement. In his historical account of vegetarianism, Colin Spencer correlates vegetarianism among the ancient Egyptians with religious piety. In ancient Egypt, animals were ritually sacrificed to the gods; thus, not to eat meat was to appropriate the behavior of the gods: "Not to eat meat, but simply to smell the aromas, was to become god-like, a sign of piety." Similar behavior existed among the especially pious early Christians who often survived on little more than bread and water—or at most a few beans and greens—as a "method by which the soul in pursuit of God dominated the wanton desire of the flesh."[48] In these cases, attempts to achieve spiritual purity through eating (or, more precisely, not eating) involve a transcendence of bodily desires and pleasures for the sake of religious belief. The denial of sacrificial meats and the rejection of all food but bread, beans, and greens inscribe spirituality in the body and become both internal and external signs of spirituality or religiosity. That is, the bodily sensation of denying cravings and desires for food constantly reinforces the strength of the individual's religious beliefs; at the same time, the effect of such abnegation manifests itself in the body's outward appearance as a sign of purity for others to read.

While attempts to achieve spiritual purity through eating no longer stem from such clearly religious motivations, the relationship between regulating diet and achieving spirituality is still a powerful one capable of furthering the commodification of macrobiotic eating. Macrobiotic eating prioritizes diet—and the macrobiotic diet in particular—as the most complete way of realizing spirituality. According to the philosophy of macrobiotics, eating the proper foods "charges" people with energy, and the more highly charged a person, the more spiritual: "When you eat the proper food, you become more highly charged. Our physical condition is equal to our spiritual condition. . . . When we eat bad food, a variety of shaky vibrations are produced and our receiver does not work properly. . . . Without eating properly, our cells will not be highly charged, and we cannot be a really spiritual person. The macrobiotic way of eating can help everyone become highly spiritualized." The philosophy of macrobiotics also perceives quantities of food as indexes of spirituality. Based on the belief that food consumption (in terms of the ratio of food weight to body weight) decreases with biological evolution, the more evolved the species, the less physical food is required for survival. Thus, as humans begin to evolve into *homo spiritus* (as Kushi and Esko predict), we will consume much less physical food, thus freeing space for a greater intake of "air and vibration, including energy from the sun, stars, and celestial bodies," much purer forms of sustenance altogether. Similarly, as people age, they have less need for physical food, though their charge still increases.[49] As was the case with the extremely pious early Christians, the ability to live on small quantities of food is both an internal and an external mark of great spirituality.

According to the macrobiotic philosophy, spiritual purity is further connected to a rejection of materialism: "There is a relationship between the volume of food we eat and the volume of material things we are attached to. The person who eats less is less attached to material things. He or she is more easily satisfied."[50] By drawing together spirituality and the rejection of materialism, the macrobiotic philosophy further distinguishes itself from mainstream American (or Western or modern) culture. Implicit in the macrobiotic exhortation to transcend both bodily and worldly attractions and attachments is a critique of modernity, and American culture in particular, a culture depicted as overindulgent, unhealthy, and spiritually vapid. One call to macrobiotic living invokes all of these ideas: "Whatever the area, cooking, learning, exercising, there is a short, instant, more 'convenient' way to do it in America. There are, however, growing numbers who seek to uncomplicate their lives from these so-called conveniences: those who wish to do their own cooking, growing, thinking and moving; those who realize that overeating, drinking, and the poor quality of food are the result of a basic ignorance of biological chemistry and the depersonalization of the food industry to the point that it hardly relates to people any longer."[51] These markers of modernity—"conveniences," "overeating," "poor quality of food"—exact a price not only on people but on the planet as well.

Even more, the costs of such a lifestyle further magnify the gap between "the natural world" and the one that sustains modernity: "A disregard for the natural world leads to plundering of the earth's resources and pollution of its atmosphere and water. A renewed commitment to the preservation of biological life and to the natural harmony between humans and nature can help us to resolve these and other problems that threaten our wholeness and our very survival."[52] Together, these two excerpts reveal the logic driving the macrobiotic rejection of the dominant American culture. The industries and technology necessary to sustain modern conveniences, to generate the abundance of food which allows for overeating, and to meet the demand for synthetic or artificial (and by some standards, poor quality) foods are also the industries and technologies which wreak havoc on the earth's resources and disregard the natural—or spiritual—world. Thus, to opt out of dominant American culture through macrobiotic living necessarily elevates one to a higher spiritual level by forging new connections with "the natural" and thus "the spiritual." New Age capitalism and the consumption of macrobiotic-related products—books, magazines, instant foods, vacations and retreats, restaurants and community centers—enable macrobiotic proselytizing and continually create new forums for pressing the return to nature and the spiritual.

Mind over Matter: Ideologies of Health and Dieting

Implicit in the positioning of macrobiotic living outside of mainstream America is also a negation of cultural eating practices and a dismissal of the cultural fixations with food as it relates to health, beauty, and sexuality. Attitudes toward food and eating in the United States are predicated on the belief in food as more than food, the belief that food can also be medicine.[53] Thus, on the one hand, food is understood as the enemy—too much cholesterol, too much fat, too much sugar, too many artificial ingredients, too many hormones, too many pesticides. On the other hand, food might be seen as the hero—the right foods can protect against a range of diseases from cancer and heart disease to osteoporosis and depression. Between the two poles are bodily desires and cravings, bodily pleasures, and bodily controls and deprivations. Reconciling the belief in food as medicine and the simultaneous desire for bodily pleasures and bodily control has generated a massive market for a variety of new food products, ranging from fat-free cheesecake and sugar-free chocolates to breads made with flaxseed oil and specialty drinks for fighting free radicals.

Science and advertising are the two greatest forces in the development and perpetuation of food-medicine fads. Together, they give rise to superfoods, foods such as oat bran, red wine, and vitamin C, capable of prolonging life and reducing the risk of diseases, at least in the popular imagination. With oat bran, perhaps the first major superfood to be identified and marketed as such in the United States, food manufacturers were so desperate to secure a share of the market that they added oat bran to their products for the sole purposes of advertising—thus, the creation of oat bran pretzels, oat bran donuts, even oat bran beer.[54] While the benefits of most superfoods are greatest when eaten in moderate amounts as part of a balanced diet, most have come to be perceived as miraculous curatives during the height of their popularity. In this sense, science and advertising appease the tension between health concerns and bodily desires for indulgent foods. That is, consumers tend to operate on the belief that oat bran for breakfast makes up for a big juicy steak, french fries, and cheesecake for dinner. A similar faith in superfoods exists in "health food" circles as well; however, these superfoods simply get less mainstream media attention and fewer advertising dollars. For instance, flaxseed oil, echinacea, and psyllium are among the elixirs extracted from their natural sources and added to everything from teas and candies to breads and sauces.

Macrobiotic eating is complicated in such food trends insofar as it epitomizes healthy eating and living. In advocating an environmentally balanced diet, however, it also removes itself from such concerns. With macrobiotics, one need not keep track of what contains oat bran, flaxseed oil, vitamin C, echinacea, psyllium, or whatever the latest superfood is because macrobiotics is a complete system for reducing the risk of disease and prolonging life. In offering a systematic approach to health and eating, macrobiotics purports to elevate itself above the health and food fads of mainstream eaters. In this sense it again positions the macrobiotic way as a more spiritual way of living, a moral way of living that can be experienced only by those who have the discipline to follow it.

Of course, a dominant subtext of the cultural fixation with food and health is the obsession with body image, particularly (but not solely) among women. Thus, fat-free foods not only reduce the risk of heart disease but also reduce the body to fit the culturally valued form. The tendency to restrict eating is as pervasive as proponents of macrobiotic eating suggest overeating and overindulgence are. According to one clinician who runs a group for people with eating disorders, "disordered eating—people who are obsessed about weight and body image" affects 80-85 percent of all women at some point during their lives.[55] Such an estimate may sound exaggerated, but a 1987 study showing that "normal" eating is now characterized by periodic—though sometimes constant—dieting and weight control.[56] As motivation for these disordered, but normative, eating practices, the researchers cite the relationship between thinness and "power, health, and other contemporary values," as well as the desire to exert control over the body.[57]

Popular, social, academic, and scientific attention to eating disorders climaxed in the 1980s as the extent of the epidemic began to surface.[58] In being exposed, disordered eating seems to have become at once acceptable and stigmatized. Constant dieting, skipping desserts, and eating fat-free substitute foods are such common practices that they draw no attention; at the same time, feminism raised awareness about eating disorders and disordered eating, and many women no longer want to pander to the body shapes and sizes valued by the dominant culture, at least not publicly. Thus, controlled eating often draws admiration—as strong commitments to any exacting regimen tend to—while also inspiring shame or embarrassment. Stacey's justification for using a pseudonym to describe one woman's personal assessment of her disordered eating typifies this paradox: "She prefers to use a pseudonym, because however dedicated she may be to her dietary regimen, she is also embarrassed by its severity." In the case of "Laurel Schiller," the tension between "enlightenment" and the desire to control the body and to fit a social ideal plays itself out in an exceptionally strict diet that contains absolutely no fat but lots of fat substitutes. After a 200-calorie dinner of salad tossed in balsamic vinegar and mustard, Schiller digs into a 370-calorie "banana split" made with a real banana and a carton of Dutch Chocolate American Glacé frozen dessert. Schiller understands that she is obsessive about her eating; she understands that it is about control. She understands that "there [is] something a little wrong with this." The reward of being a size 6 and exerting some order in her life outweighs these other considerations.[59]

Supporters of the macrobiotic way cannot be ignorant of disordered eating and its prevalence in the United States. The philosophy and practice of macrobiotic eating, however, necessarily rejects such a relationship with food as it disregards the primary principles of the diet—to eat according to nature, in harmony with the environment, and until sated. Thus, transcending the fixations with food characteristic of contemporary eating practices in the United States becomes another way in which macrobiotic eating can distinguish itself from the dominant culture.

And yet macrobiotic eating is still deeply implicated in and frequently exploits the concerns with the body that may contribute to eating disorders. For instance, *The Macrobiotic Way*—a classic text in the philosophy and practice of macrobiotic living—sells the philosophy as a means of controlling body weight and shape by describing the struggle that many people have in maintaining "normal" weight. According to this source, most people gain an extra fourteen pounds of fat between the ages of twenty-five and forty; to help the reader personalize the annual increase of one pound of fat, the authors break it down into a daily consumption of an extra forty calories or one extra teaspoon of sugar. Typical weight-loss diets are then contrasted with the macrobiotic diet: "Unlike the foods that comprise the popular high-protein weight-loss diets, which tend to drain energy and stimulate cravings for sweets, the complex carbohydrates in the macrobiotic diet reduce cravings for sweets and other fattening foods, and provide plenty of energy as well."[60] Here, Michio Kushi's and Stephen Blauer's tactic of criticizing other diets as a way of upholding the macrobiotic approach to weight loss is a common one. Because most dieters are chronic dieters, they are aware of different approaches to weight loss and have likely tried a number of diets. Since regular dieting tends to involve cycles of success and failure, criticizing other diets is likely to resonate with readers who understand on a bodily and experiential level that other diets (or, more likely, all diets) involve cravings for forbidden foods. In this way, the dieter's own experiences enhance the credibility of the macrobiotic approach to weight loss.

Kushi and Blauer further sell the macrobiotic approach to weight loss by invoking common diet discourse: "Losing weight and then maintaining the desired weight is not difficult on the macrobiotic diet. . . . Depending on how much you weigh now and the extent to which you adhere to macrobiotic principles, your weight should normalize in a matter of days, weeks, or months. . . . On the macrobiotic diet, as long as you eat until satisfied, two to three times per day, you will meet your bodily nutritional needs." The promises of weight loss and maintenance, quick weight loss, and eating until satisfied are the cornerstones of all diets. Advertisements for weight-loss programs like Jenny Craig, Weight Watchers, and LA Weight Loss Centers as well as for weight-loss products like diet pills and diet shakes all rely on these three appeals. Testimonials from those who have supposedly succeeded in losing weight through such regimens are another common feature of popular diet discourse, and their narrative power is not lost on those advocating the macrobiotic diet as a weight-loss strategy. An example in one book refers to one man's quick and drastic weight loss: "As in William Duffy's case, fifty or more pounds lost over a period of months is not uncommon. . . . You can generally expect to lose about one to three pounds a week."[61]

Thus, despite efforts to transcend the dominant cultural fixations with food as it relates to health and body image, macrobiotics is firmly entrenched in discourses of diets and disordered eating. Within the macrobiotic community, issues of body image and weight loss frequently become dangerous obsessions. In a *Macrobiotics Today* article titled "It's Your Metabolism, Not Your Diet," Z'ev Rosenberg draws attention to these issues and particularly to the tendency for people to equate "the image of health" with "the slender macrobiotic leader (who may, in reality, not be all so healthy)." Such an equation generates a pressure to conform to the leader's slender image in order to signal—both internally and externally—the correct practice of macrobiotics; however, Rosenberg contends that focusing on the image rather than the practice can result in "eating too yang or too strictly in an attempt to acquire this slender image of health." He also points out that women, in particular, often have a difficult time losing weight on the macrobiotic diet (though he doesn't say why) and consequently become frustrated and obsessive, treating it like the mass of other "crash diets and strenuous exercise regimens." Rosenberg's critique of diets and the macrobiotic emphasis on superficial slenderness would seem in concert with the macrobiotic philosophy of eating harmoniously and living in balance with nature, a philosophy which prioritizes the practice more than the product. Yet, Rosenberg concludes his article by offering a better way to achieve and maintain the body's ideal weight. He suggests "awakening the body's innate intelligence" and learning as much about oneself, cooking, and foods as possible. Together, these suggestions enact the macrobiotic diet without placing too much emphasis on body image; as a result, "the body will adjust to its proper constitutional needs and settle into its natural weight. This is all that should be necessary to treat any weight problem."[62] The suggestion that the body can achieve its "natural" weight through macrobiotic eating and the implication that such a natural weight corresponds to a lean physique typifies the macrobiotic attitude toward weight loss and the body. In essence, the philosophy of macrobiotics rejects dominant cultural concerns with food as medicine and eating as relates to body image and posits a "purer," more "natural" way of attaining the same goals. Nonetheless, references to healthy, lean macrobiotic eaters abound in the literature.

The commodification of macrobiotic eating depends, in part, on its participation in mainstream discourses of health and dieting, superfoods and super bodies, which ultimately fragments mind and body. Common to macrobiotic eating, "healthy" superfood eating, and dieting and restricted eating are issues of control. All three of these ways of eating involve a certain mental control over the body, an ongoing process of food choices based not on bodily desires for food—or even the desire for bodily and gustatory pleasure—but rather on a system of beliefs about diet, health, beauty, and power. This basic control of the body is then multiplied outward. For people with eating disorders, control—and not body image—is often the primary concern. The ability to control eating and the body is also a way of compensating for lack of control over other aspects of life. Laurel Schiller describes this relationship in talking about her extreme regimen for eating: "For a long time I just didn't want to go out much because I was worried about what I'd eat. That's when I realized there was something a little wrong with this—that it probably had a lot to do with control. Aaron [her fiancé] moving out was completely out of my control, and it was so awful. . . . This eating thing showed I really was in control. It felt good."[63] Similar attitudes characterize macrobiotic eating. As macrobiotic cookbook authors Barbara Rossi and Glory Schloss imply, macrobiotic living often takes on the qualities of monkish asceticism, a lifestyle that has come to symbolize an extreme level of restriction and control.

In addition to controlling lifestyle and eating, the macrobiotic philosophy also offers the diet as a means of controlling health, life, and death: "Remember that death is an act of will. . . . We die only by our ignorance and our will. People choose the manner and time of their death. There is no reason to die at seventy or eighty years of age. If you want to live longer, you can do so with your understanding of the principles of macrobiotics."[64] Here, Kushi and Esko equate "being" with the "will" and imply that the will is situated in the mind. As such, it has the ability to control the physical body, to keep it from dying until it sees fit. Regardless of whether the desire for control is simply a fin-de-siècle phenomenon as Stacey suggests,[65] the effect of such control is a separation of mind and body in a way that undermines the holistic philosophy of macrobiotic living.

Subtle distinctions between physical body and mind exist throughout the macrobiotic literature. For instance, in describing the period required to purify oneself through macrobiotics, Kushi and Esko allot different times for physical purification as opposed to emotional purification: "Eating macrobiotically for seven years will establish your physical condition, but to purify your memory takes seven times seven years of proper eating."[66] In the macrobiotic scheme of things, this notion implies that the mind is far superior to the body.

This hierarchical distinction between mind and body is further reinforced through the common mechanistic metaphors of the body in the macrobiotic discourse. In one case, the body is referred to as "the body-machine,"[67] though such models of the body are usually not so blatant. Book, cookbook, and testimonial descriptions of the effects of the macrobiotic diet on the body frequently invoke such imagery. For instance, Dick Benedict describes his decision to treat a tumor in his prostate with macrobiotic eating: "I was not scared because I had been studying macrobiotics, and I believed completely in the principles behind it. Actually, I was excited by the adventure of it. Growing up in Montana, I learned: If the tractor breaks down, fix it. So I always have had that in my nature."[68] Here, Benedict's analogy between his body and a tractor makes explicit the mechanistic understanding of the body underlying the macrobiotic philosophy. In another instance, Kushi and Esko compare the body's functioning to that of a television set (a somewhat ironic comparison considering that the macrobiotic way advises against having a television); according to the analogy, in order to receive the most vibrations from the universe, the television/body must have the best possible receiver. Macrobiotic eating tunes the receiver and allows it to obtain the most vibrations.[69] More frequently, the macrobiotic diet is presented as fuel which helps the body/machine run most efficiently: "Compared to proteins or fats, complex carbohydrates provide the body with more easily usable fuel for energy, and leave behind fewer waste products. . . . The mainstays of the macrobiotic diet, on the other hand, are clean-burning complex carbohydrates."[70] The language of fuel, energy, and waste products thoroughly reinforces the image of the body as a modern machine. Through the popular discourses of macrobiotics, the body becomes a machine to be altered and fixed by a certain mental or spiritual transcendence. In upholding the body as raw material to be fixed, trimmed, and altered, the macrobiotic philosophy grants the very essence of being to the mind and the will, to the ability to transcend the bodily desires and cravings and pains as part of a spiritual undertaking.

Other Foods, Other Bodies

The commodification of macrobiotic eating derives much of its power from the continual act of distancing itself from the same mainstream American culture that it draws upon for its metaphors, whether in terms of dominant cultural eating practices and fixations with food or in terms of attitudes toward spirituality, materialism, technology, and nature. Such distancing is perhaps most evident in the macrobiotic representations of otherness upon which the whole philosophy of living is premised. Although the origins of macrobiotics are most frequently attributed to Hippocrates, the current macrobiotic movement looks to Japan as its point of origin. Thus, the "traditional" foods upon which the macrobiotic diet is based are traditional Japanese foods, and many of the staples, condiments, and supplementary foods as well as the styles of preparing and cooking them are Japanese. The commodification of macrobiotic eating in the United States also means the commercialization of Japanese food products and the mimesis of Japanese culinary traditions, both of which draw upon and augment the exoticization and consumption of the Japanese body.

General distinctions between East and West establish a pattern for the ways in which conceptualizations of otherness are invoked and frequently essentialized by celebration throughout the macrobiotic literature. Ohsawa, the founder of the current macrobiotic movement, defines macrobiotics through exactly this type of East-West contrast: "[Macrobiotics] is a different kind of medicine, totally unknown in the West until recently. . . . This medicine has a history of more than five thousand years. It is a physiological application of the dialectic principle of life that has been totally ignored even in Japan since the importation of Western civilization about a century ago."[71] Here, the Eastern conception of health—based on the dialectic principle of life—is upheld as superior to Western medicine because of its five-thousand-year history. Thus, just as the "traditional" diet is better than the "modern" diet because of its closer connection to nature and the environment, so too is the "traditional" understanding of health better than the "modern" or Western understanding of it.

The characterization of the East as natural, particularly in contrast to the West, is one that pervades the macrobiotic literature. Another example makes the association explicit: "The natural way to life is the joyous way of life. The alternative to industrialized, chemicalized food, stagnating inactivity and pills for everything are pure and simple food, yoga and exercise, and healing the natural way with herbs. We Westerners would do well to take a few lessons from our Eastern contemporaries, who, although influenced by Western modes of eating, drinking and living, have still managed to preserve a certain amount of traditional knowledge concerning the art of eating healthfully."[72] In heralding the triumph of Eastern traditions over the evil influences of the West, proponents of the macrobiotic way also relegate contemporary Japan—as the macrobiotic symbol of "the East"—to a distant past. The process of temporal distancing creates "objects or referents of anthropological discourse," and in creating objects of any type of discourse about ethnic Others, temporal distancing also denies the Other any voice as an equal participant in conversation.[73] Thus, contemporary Japanese people—like the Hunza, the Vilcabambans, and the Abkhasians—become icons of a lost past, symbolic representations of the "natural" and the "traditional." Moreover, implicit in such descriptions is the celebration of the hegemony of Western modernity.[74] The very commemoration of and nostalgia for the "traditional" suggests a social evolutionary model which places the modern societies of the West at the peak; so powerful is the influence of the West that it has disrupted five thousand years of tradition in the East.

Against these general East-West contrasts and enmeshed in the macrobiotic discourse of health and eating are more specific distinctions between Japanese bodies and Western bodies. The "Japanese body" is frequently upheld as an exemplar of health, particularly when contrasted with the typical "American body." For instance, a common practice in the macrobiotic literature is to cite epidemiological studies in which the Japanese rates for lung cancer, breast cancer, and colorectal cancer are drastically lower than the American equivalents, a variance attributed largely to dietary differences.[75] The reasons for these differences tend to fall into two categories: dietary fat levels and the use of specific Japanese "traditional" foods. The level of daily fat intake—a possible determinant of cancer—is much lower among Japanese. At the same time, specific foods like soy products, fermented products, sea vegetables, and fiber all seem to reduce the risk of certain cancers in laboratory animals.[76] In essence, the macrobiotic philosophy follows a transitive logic whereby macrobiotic eating translates into the Japanese diet, and the Japanese diet results in lower cancer rates or lower incidences of heart disease, obesity, even postnasal drip;[77] therefore, the macrobiotic diet leads to greater health as embodied by Japanese people.

Contrasts between Japanese bodies and American bodies are frequently invoked as justification for the macrobiotic way. For instance, in recommending against the consumption of milk and dairy foods,

Kushi and Blauer bolster their warning against such foods with biological evidence: "Recent research published in *Diet, Nutrition, and Cancer*, a National Academy of Sciences report, has linked the fats in dairy products to an increase in the presence of cysts and tumors of the breast, uterus, and ovaries in American women. Japanese women, who rarely consume dairy foods, and who eat fewer saturated fats, have a lower incidence of these problems."[78] While examples like this make the health of Japanese bodies an explicit goal of the macrobiotic way, more implicit references to the "macrobiotic" body make the physical shape of the Japanese body an object of desire. For example, those who eat macrobiotically are said to weigh ten to twenty pounds less than the average recommended for their heights.

While this may not be an ideal body image for everyone, it is for many. For many women, and probably some men, the recommended weights are often perceived as high. Many women would prefer to be "thin-thin" as opposed to being just thin or, even worse, being "average": "'Thin-thin' is a conjunction that comes up often in her [Laurel Schiller's] patter about food. It seems to denote just the right level of thin—not merely a kind of natural slenderness, which is what Laurel has had most of her life but which is a size 8 rather than a size 6; thin-thin is something that works with clingy black skirts or tight stretch pants."[79] Indeed, Laurel Schiller's fixation with "thin-thin," with the size 6 body, is part of a trend that has set new standards beyond any nutritional, health, or insurance guidelines defining the average body. Implicit in her descriptions of what the size 6 body can wear—and thus what it can do and what it can accomplish—is the power of the gaze, the complicated dance of desire and (self)objectification.

A less specific description of the macrobiotic body makes it even more desirable, as it leaves the precise details open to the reader's imagination and individual preferences: "Eating macrobiotically leads to a more yang appearance; the body becomes slimmer, with better muscle definition and more graceful contours."[80] Anyone concerned with his or her body image cannot deny the attraction of a body with "more graceful contours." The "thin-thin" body is also the "slimmer" body, the body with more clearly defined muscles, the macrobiotic body, and the macrobiotic body is the essentialized and objectified Japanese body created by the macrobiotic discourse. The association between the macrobiotic body and the Japanese body is not unique to the macrobiotic literature; rather, the macrobiotic literature draws on a legacy of stereotypes and stereotyped representations of the Asian body—small, petite, slender, lean; never bulky, obese, fat, large. Together with these images of the Asian body, the popular discourses of macrobiotic eating continue to remake the stereotypes, thereby continually granting them power.[81]

The literature on macrobiotic living has drawn on science and stereotype to create an object of desire in the Japanese body. The commodification of macrobiotic eating promises the physical condition—both internal and external—of the Japanese body through a bodily ethnomimesis. To eat Japanese foods, cooked according to Japanese principles, using Japanese kitchen utensils is to live a Japanese life. When ethnomimesis is enacted in such a physical way, when it is literally taken into the body, the cultural consumption inherent in any such act of imitation takes on a more literal significance. It is not just a Japanese meal which is consumed; rather, it is an iconically Japanese way of life, an essentialized attitude, a stereotyped physicality.

Conclusion

It is through the process of commodification that macrobiotic eating has emerged as a systematic approach to health and living. The ingredients and utensils necessary for living the macrobiotic way are available in most health food stores, including larger health-oriented "supermarkets" like the Whole Foods chain (owner of Bread and Circus, Fresh Fields, and Wild Oats) as well as through specialty catalogues and webpages. The ongoing—and constant—process of transforming macrobiotic practices into macrobiotic products is frequently conflated with educational efforts such that Kushi Cuisine "quick" foods offer a brief history and philosophy of macrobiotic living on each product package and macrobiotic cooking classes in a Philadelphia health food store are aired on public television. Here, the process and project of New Age capitalism slowly moves the fringe into the mainstream.

Where macrobiotic eating is concerned, people need not force themselves into a lifestyle which is constantly being threatened by other choices, by the dominant cultural practices of eating in an average restaurant, indulging in food cravings, even eating for the sheer bodily and gustatory pleasure of it. To take advantage of what macrobiotic eating has to offer—or at least to have the impression of doing so—one need only buy a macrobiotic cookbook and prepare a meal, visit the local ashram, or even dine at the Ritz-Carlton, which now offers more than one hundred macrobiotic options on its complete menu program.[82]

4

YOGA AND T'AI CHI

Despite the fact that yoga and t'ai chi are distinctly different in practice, origin, and philosophy, the two popular activities have been linked conceptually in the public imagination. In addition, the public sphere discourse devoted to alternative health and wellness sustains and naturalizes this link between the two. Television and radio programs, newspaper and magazine articles, health club and recreation department offerings, spa vacations and exercise retreats, even catalogues for clothing devoted to alternative exercise all bring yoga and t'ai chi together. Insofar as both are "alternative," somewhat exoticized means of spirituality, mind-body integration, relaxation and stress release, as well as staying well, building strength, and transforming the body's shape, they are presented as interchangeable means of fulfilling the same goal.

Yoga and t'ai chi involve bodily mimesis on a much more extensive and literal level than macrobiotic eating and aromatherapy. The traditionalization and commodification of yoga and t'ai chi—and the bodily mimesis implicit in the Westernized forms—allow the individual practitioner to make his or her own body foreign, to make it other. Yet at the same time, the relevant promises of bodily (and sometimes spiritual) transformation are packaged within the context of dominant ideologies of the body. Thus, the body is made foreign to make it fit the familiar, to become the culturally valued shape, strength, size. Through yoga and t'ai chi, individuals are equipped—and almost obliged—to address issues of the self, modernity, and globalization through personal practice. As with aromatherapy and macrobiotic eating, the personal and the political come together within the context of modernity and individualism.

From Philosophy to Physicality

Yoga and t'ai chi are two philosophies that join physical and mental exercise as a way of achieving enlightenment and harmony with the universe.[1] Both trace their roots to classical Eastern religious texts—the classical texts of India for yoga and the classical texts of China for t'ai chi. In uncovering, identifying, and creating such origins and legacies, contemporary popular American forms of yoga and t'ai chi traditionalize the activities, thereby forging histories that imply a certain continuity with ancient practices. Despite the fact that neither yoga nor t'ai chi has been performed continually since classical periods, the traditionalization of these practices often provides the mystique that attracts modern practitioners seeking alternative ways of living. As first commodified and subsequently practiced in the United States and many other countries around the world, yoga and t'ai chi are removed from their philosophical contexts and largely undertaken as physical exercise regimens, though still presented within the context of body-mind integration and spirituality. In essence, the physical elements of the philosophical systems have come to represent—and be—what we call yoga and t'ai chi.

Yoga

The word *yoga* is common throughout Sanskrit literature and derives from the verbal root *yuj,* which means to bind or to yoke, a meaning which takes on many connotations such as "union, conjunction of stars, grammatical rule, endeavor, occupation, team, equipment, means, trick, magic, aggregate, [and] sum." Philosophically, yoga refers to the various paths to self-unification and the "transformation of consciousness" necessary to achieve such a union.[2]

Some have traced yoga back as far as the Indus civilization (c. 3000–2000 B.C.E.), citing archaeological evidence from steatite seals depicting horned deities sitting in typical yoga fashion. Of particular interest is the *pásupati*-seal, which portrays a seated divinity surrounded by four animals—an elephant, a tiger, a rhinoceros, and a buffalo. Beneath the seat are two antelopes. The figure is commonly believed to be Siva, the lord of the beasts and the "arch-*yogin.*"[3] However, such evidence is highly speculative and inconclusive.

Slightly less speculative evidence exists in the *Ṛg Veda* (c. 1500–1000 B.C.E.) where the word *yoga* seems to refer to "yoga-like practices and concepts," though these references are also open to controversy.[4] Many of the yoga-like practices and concepts mentioned in the *Ṛg Veda* overlap with shamanistic practices, and Mircea Eliade is cautious in identifying these practices only as a "protean yoga."[5] Other evidence from the *Vedas* occurs in *vrātya-khaṇḍa* (book XV) of the *Atharvaveda*. The vrātyas were nomads who traveled throughout the northeast of India and existed outside of orthodox vedic society. While they were looked down upon and were often victims of human sacrifice, their numbers and social power were such that they were eventually accepted into the vedic community through special rites introduced by the orthodox priesthood. The *vrātya-khaṇḍa* suggests that the vrātyas lived ascetically and practiced *prāṇāyāma*, a means of focusing the life force in order to channel transcendental power and transform consciousness, a process common to later forms of yoga and to Tantrism.[6]

Many of these early yoga practices and concepts had begun to crystallize by the time of the Buddha in the sixth century B.C.E. The Buddha was himself a yogi committed to meditation, and he saw in yoga a way out of the "maze of sorrowful existence," particularly through meditative absorption and enstasy, the total unification of self and consciousness. The Buddha's system of yoga involves eight distinct aspects, five of which are socio-ethical regulations and three of which are expressly yogic. The three specifically yogic aspects include *samma-vayama* ("right exertion" or the controlling of emotional response to external conditions), *samma-sati* ("right mindfulness" or the awareness of psychosomatic processes), and *samma-samādhi* ("right unification" or the practice of internalizing consciousness; in the Buddha's system of yoga, there are also eight phases of unification ranging from sense-withdrawal to enstasy).[7] In addition, the Buddha also incorporated such techniques as *āsana* (postures) and *prāṇāyāma*, the two aspects of yoga which are most commonly practiced in the United States today.

The development of yoga is more clearly articulated in the oldest portions of the *Mahābhārata*, particularly the *Bhagavad-Gītā*, and in the secondary, or middle, *Upaniṣads* (500-300 B.C.E.), including the *Kaṭha-*, *Śvetāśvatara-*, *Īśa-*, and *Muṇḍaka-Upaniṣads*.[8] The *Bhagavad-Gītā* (chapters 13-40 of the sixth book of the *Mahābhārata*) offers one of the first explicit references to yoga as a practice aimed at emancipation from eternal existence through continual re-embodiments as well as the achievement of union with the Supreme Being. Though written down sometime in the second or third century B.C.E., the *Mahābhārata* was composed and orally transmitted over several centuries. The specific yoga movements mentioned in the epic predate the literary version, as is evident from the fact that the Buddha consulted two teachers who subscribed to some of the traditions elaborated in the epic. However, the specific schools mentioned in the *Mahābhārata* are post-buddhist, most likely dating between 500 and 200 B.C.E.[9]

In the *Bhagavad-Gītā*, the god Krishna encourages a balance between spiritual asceticism and worldly religion and ethics, and this idea of renunciation (*saṃnyāsa*) in action is the ideal of *karma-yoga*. Yet Krishna's yoga goes further than later yoga practices, and he essentially advocates that everything in one's daily life be realigned to the Supreme Being: "One's whole life must become a continual yoga." Consequently, Krishna yoga involves several forms of contemporary yoga, including *jñāna-yoga* (yoga of gnostic knowledge), *karma-yoga* (yoga of ethical action), and *bhakti-yoga* (yoga of devotion to the Divine). The yoga scholar Georg Feuerstein describes Krishna yoga as "integral Yoga."[10]

The secondary *Upaniṣads* provide loose guidelines for various yoga techniques and for the yogic principle of involution, a process through which an individual achieves higher levels of being through increased consciousness. By the third century B.C.E. when the *Maitrāyaṇīya-Upaniṣad* (c. 300 B.C.E.) is believed to have been composed, yoga had become a much more developed philosophy and practice. This scripture provides very specific information about yoga techniques, particularly the use of the sacred syllable *oṃ*. In addition, the *Maitrāyaṇīya-Upaniṣad* elaborates a six-member yoga (the six practices necessary to realize the bliss of the Supreme Lord), which seems to be a precursor to the standard eight-member yoga later systematized by Patañjali in the classic *Yoga-sūtras*. Of the six members mentioned in the *Maitrāyaṇīya-Upaniṣad*, only five are consistent with the later eight-member system of Patañjali; absent are the *āsanas* (poses) and the ethical precepts (*yama* and *niyama*). The sixth element, absent from the eight-member system of the *Yoga-sūtras*, is *tarka* (reasoned reflection), which might correspond with a type of enstasy in which analytical thinking is still possible.[11] Though the secondary *Upaniṣads* and the *Bhagavad-Gītā* present this wide range of yogic philosophy and technique, they do not articulate the principles of yoga in any systematic fashion as Patañjali later did in the *Yoga-sūtras*.

The long and diffuse development of classical yoga culminates in the second or third century C.E. with Patañjali's *Yoga-sūtras*, a text that soon established the authoritative yoga tradition and still provides the basis for virtually all schools of yoga.[12] The *Yoga-sūtras* bring together yoga theory and practice in the form of 195 aphorisms (*sūtra*), which are divided into four chapters:

(1) *samādhi-pāda*, chapter on enstasy	51 aphorisms
(2) *sādhanā-pāda*, chapter on the path	55 aphorisms
(3) *vibhūti-pāda*, chapter on the powers	55 aphorisms
(4) *kaivalya-pāda*, chapter on emancipation	34 aphorisms[13]

Together, these aphorisms outline a method for "the systematic transformation of consciousness with the ultimate purpose of achieving 'liberation' or 'Self realisation.'" Implicit in this method and in the aphorisms is Patañjali's philosophy of yoga which concerns itself with the possibility of all knowledge or "root consciousness." Despite the fact that Patañjali's *Yoga-sūtras* join yoga theory with practice, the text has most frequently been upheld for its practical applications. Thus, while scholars of Indian religion and philosophy contend that the section on *aṣṭāṅga-yoga* (the eight-fold path to enlightenment; literally, "yoga of eight members") is subordinate to the more philosophical section on *kriya-yoga*, it is the *aṣṭāṅga* section that most commonly classifies the *Yoga-sūtras*.[14] The eight-fold path builds upon the earlier six elements described in the *Maitrāyaṇīya-Upaniṣad*; specifically, the eight members are *yama* (general ethical principles), *niyama* (principles of self-restraint), *āsana* (the postures for meditation), *prāṇāyāma* (breathing techniques), *pratyāhāra* (sense-withdrawal), *dhāraṇā* (concentration), *dhyāna* (meditative absorption), and *samādhi* (enstasy).[15]

Several distinct yoga traditions eventually developed from the *Yoga-sūtras*, but they all continue to rely on Patañjali's techniques for the basis of their practice. Among the five most popular and prominent schools of yoga are *rāja* yoga, *haṭha* yoga, *jñāna* yoga, *bhakti* yoga, and *karma* yoga. *Rāja* yoga is a predominantly intellectual form of yoga, also known as "the royal yoga," and most frequently contrasted with the primarily physical *haṭha* yoga. The main objective of *rāja* yoga is to transcend mental activity such that consciousness may realize a state of deep meditative absorption. The more physical *haṭha* yoga, on the other hand, seeks to achieve immortality through a transformation of the physical body into the divine body; however, *haṭha* yoga is not concerned only with the physical body but also with an individual's many layers of being. In essence, *haṭha* yoga is premised on the idea that transcendence can only occur through a healthy body. *Jñāna* yoga emphasizes the acquisition of intuitive knowledge as a way of discerning differences between the real and the unreal, the finite and the infinite. *Bhakti* yoga is a devotional form of yoga and is characterized by the "supreme attachment to the Lord." The goal of *bhakti* yoga is to achieve a passionate and ecstatic love for God; in so doing, all barriers between the devotee and God are removed, and the devotee "perceives the entire cosmos to be penetrated by the presence of God" while also experiencing unity with God. *Karma* yoga is a yoga of action, specifically spirituality based on selfless action; thus, transcendence is possible through acts of selflessness as well as those "performed without any self-interest."[16]

Themes of liberation and transcendence run through all of these yoga traditions and stem from the classic yoga as systematized in Patañjali's *Yoga-sūtras*; historically, the yoga traditions of these five schools were transmitted individually from guru to student, and all of the schools had roughly equal numbers of followers. Today, in India as well as around the world, *haṭha* yoga is the predominant yoga tradition, most frequently in its primarily physical form and thus removed—at least explicitly—from the ultimate goals of transcendence and emancipation.

The international rise of *haṭha* yoga is attributed to one man, B. K. S. Iyengar, who began teaching to groups of students in colleges and schools in India in the late 1930s. During the early 1930s, *haṭha* yoga was undergoing a popular renaissance in India as a small number of yogis began to adapt some of the ancient teachings for secular audiences and then offered them, for the first time, to the general public.[17] Among the teachers responsible for the secularization of yoga was Iyengar's brother-in-law, Krishnamacharya, a renowned Sanskrit scholar and practicing yogi who founded a yoga school under the patronage of the Maharaja of Mysore. At the time, Iyengar was a sickly teenager living with his sister and Krishnamacharya, who eventually taught him several poses for demonstration at an all-India World YMCA conference. After teaching in Krishnamacharya's yoga school for several years, Iyengar met Dr. V. B. Gokhale, a medical doctor who invited him to Pune to introduce yoga to the local colleges and schools. Iyengar claims to be the first person in the world to teach yoga to groups of students (as opposed to individual instruction) in such settings. Through his own practice of working through his illnesses and stiff body, through his relationship with Dr. Gokhale, and through his work with people suffering from a range of medical conditions, Iyengar began to develop a system of yoga that incorporates props to help students achieve the bodily benefits of *haṭha* yoga when they are unable to perfect the pose.

Iyengar's system of yoga (now commonly known as Iyengar yoga) spread west through his contact with Yehudi Menuhin, the celebrated violinist, who sought out Iyengar for instruction during one of Menuhin's concerts in India in the early 1950s; Menuhin later invited Iyengar to teach in Switzerland. According to Iyengar, however, it wasn't until the late 1960s that the West fully embraced *haṭha* yoga: "Yoga became very popular in the West only after 1967 or '68. In 1954 not even one student was willing to come to a demonstration of mine. . . . It took me several years to build up classes in England—it was not so easy to come to the masses. . . . Then, in 1968, fortunately, Peter Macintosh, the physical director of the London adult education center, wanted to replace calisthenic exercises with some others that would be more effective. And he was a friend of Mr. Menuhin."[18] By the mid-1970s, Iyengar yoga was widely practiced in the West, and today it is probably the most common system of *haṭha* yoga in the world.[19]

Iyengar is only partly correct in his contention that yoga became very popular in the West only after 1967 or 1968. In 1893, Swami Vivekananda arrived in Chicago to represent India, and Hinduism in particular, at the World's Parliament of Religions organized in conjunction with the Columbian Exposition; his reception was so great that he was encouraged (and funded) to deliver lectures throughout the country.[20] After nearly two years of such touring, Vivekananda settled in New York, where he founded the Vedānta Society of America. The teachings of the Vedānta Society were premised on the traditions of the *jñāna* and *rāja* schools of yoga, especially the use of meditation and the acquisition of knowledge as means of suppressing the body and attaining higher consciousness. The Vedānta Society continued to flourish with the support of wealthy society leaders, particularly women, as well as noted actresses, singers, and musicians. With such a support base, Vivekananda began to train Americans to carry on the work in Vedānta centers throughout the country, and in the late 1890s he also began to preach the tenets of *bhakti* and *karma* yoga, the yoga traditions of devotion and work. As the philosopher Wendell Thomas suggests, this transition from a tradition of asceticism and meditation to a tradition of devotion and work may reflect Vivekananda's true understanding of American religious appeal: "Now that he had gained some experience as a Western minister, he exalted the notion of work." Vivekananda continued to open Vedānta Centers in the West, expanding to England and the European Continent as well. Yet it was in California at the turn of the century that Vivekananda found the greatest support for the *rāja* yoga that he first preached upon his arrival in the United States. He felt that Californians were especially well suited for the intuitive meditation at the core of *rāja* yoga, which he labeled "Applied Psychology," and he established several more Vedānta centers in the San Francisco Bay Area.[21]

Though Vivekananda and the members of the Vedānta Society look to yoga as the foundational philosophy of their movement, their ultimate goal is not self-realization, individual emancipation, or the personal transformation of consciousness but rather pan-religious tolerance and understanding. One preacher from the Vedānta Center in New York City, Swami Jnanesvarananda, contended in 1928 that through the four types of yoga shared by the Vedānta Society—*jñāna, rāja, bhakti,* and *karma*—America can be filled "with the spirit of Vedānta, which is the spirit of the eternal, universal religion of understanding and tolerance."[22] Thus, this early tradition of yoga in the United States is grounded much more in philosophy and religion than in practice and poses, and in this way it reflects a continuation of the earlier movements of Transcendentalism (organized around 1830), Christian Science (founded 1879), and Theosophy (founded 1875), which were heavily influenced by Indian philosophy and religion.

Midway between the philosophical teachings of Vivekananda and the Vedānta Society and the physical practice of Iyengar is the work of Yogananda, founder of the Self-Realization Fellowship. Like Vivekananda, Yogananda came to the United States as the Indian delegate to the International Congress of Religious Liberals in America, and similar to Vivekananda, he established a church and toured the country lecturing to audiences large and small.[23] After several years of such lecturing and several years back in India, he settled into his seaside retreat in Encinitas, California (indeed, he too must have found Californians to be most amenable to the philosophy and practice of yoga).

Yogananda taught the basic techniques of yoga and meditation, and more than the other traditions of yoga practiced in the West, his yoga attempts to incorporate all eight limbs of Patañjali's *Yoga-sūtras*. To his particularly committed followers Yogananda also imparted the secret tradition of *kriya* yoga, a method of meditation and breath control through which "human evolution can be quickened" thereby allowing practitioners to discover the secret of cosmic consciousness.[24] Yogananda's disciples have carried on his tradition, and the Self-Realization Fellowship continues to spread his philosophy and techniques of yoga, primarily through instructional materials like books, recordings, and magazines, as well as through retreats and communes. In general, because initiation into *kriya* yoga requires twice-daily meditation, followers of this tradition tend to view yoga as a complete lifestyle, and many opt to surround themselves with other practitioners by living in communal housing arrangements and small villages.[25]

Iyengar is not ignorant of this tradition of missionary work from India to the United States. In fact, he holds a certain respect for Vivekananda; however, he points out that the yoga spread by Indian missionaries in America was largely philosophical and consequently unable to inspire widespread practice: "People can criticize me, but if I had not worked so much, would yoga have become popular? A hundred years of yoga in America—but after Vivekananda, it was sleeping. I have respect for him. He gave the teachings. But what happened afterwards? How many years passed before people began to practice? There are so many people who have come to America from India as yogis. What did they do? House to house I have introduced it."[26] Here, the ambiguity of the very concept of yoga comes to the fore. Iyengar clearly considers the physical practice the most essential aspect of yoga while others, like those involved with the Self-Realization Fellowship, perceive yoga as a complete lifestyle. What we have come to understand popularly as yoga is largely the physical yoga introduced to the West by Iyengar in the late 1960s and early 1970s. Moreover, as yoga has become more firmly entrenched in American culture, the orientation has become more and more physical. Since the late 1960s and early 1970s, interest in yoga has continued to expand. The growing number of popular magazine and newspaper articles as well as radio and television transcripts (from the Lexis/Nexis database) indicates a steady increase in interest in yoga, with a steep acceleration beginning in the late 1980s and early 1990s. Similar trends hold true for t'ai chi as well.

T'ai Chi

As is the case with yoga, the origins of t'ai chi are unknown. In one popular legend, the system of t'ai chi was imparted to the Taoist immortal Chang San-feng as he slept. Through his dream he learned the fundamental movements of t'ai chi chuan (the "Supreme, Ultimate Way of the Fist") and upon awakening realized that he was to share his new knowledge. Traveling through a village that was under attack by raiding brigands, he seized the opportunity to demonstrate his new art, transforming "an art of gentleness into an art of devastation."[27]

Perhaps the most common legend of Chang San-feng and the origins of t'ai chi involves a battle between a snake and a crane. In this legend, Chang was meditating in his hut when he was distracted by an uproarious noise outside his window. When he went to investigate, he saw that a snake and a crane were engaged in battle. The snake and the crane continually attacked each other while defending themselves until they had tired of the struggle. Each left the scene, and there was no clear winner. In the movements of the snake and the crane, Chang understood that the "soft could overcome the hard from the suppleness and pliability of the snake's circuitous movements" and that quickness and change were vital in martial arts. Thus, according to the legend, Chang derived the principles and the movements of t'ai chi from the battle between the snake and the crane, and the names of certain movements reflect this legacy—Crane Spreads Her Wings and Snake Creeps Down.[28]

Whether Chang ever existed outside of legend is unknown. Some believe that he was born toward the end of the Sung dynasty (late thirteenth century); by other accounts, he lived during the Yuan dynasty (1278–1368). Because of the conflicting dates, some scholars suggest that there was more than one Chang. At the same time, however, he is believed to have lived in his physical body for over two hundred years, so it is possible that he could have lived during both of these dynasties. He was also a practitioner of Taoist yoga and meditation, and after years of practice he eventually became one with Tao.[29] Chang was known for his exceptional build and size (he was over seven feet tall) as well as for his gracefulness and compassion. It seems that he himself was an embodiment of the t'ai chi principle of power through gentleness.

Regardless of whether Chang was real or imagined, tracing the origins of t'ai chi to him proves somewhat problematic from a historical point of view due to a gap of three to four hundred years between his life and the life of Wang Tsung-yueh, the man most frequently credited as the next link in the development of t'ai chi.[30] Nonetheless, Wang is generally acknowledged as the first known successor to Chang as well as the author of "T'ai Chi Ch'uan Lun," the most philosophical of the *T'ai Chi Classics*, a compilation of the early philosophical and instructional texts relating to t'ai chi.[31] Perhaps more important to the history of t'ai chi, however, is the legend in which Wang teaches t'ai chi to the Ch'en family in the eighteenth century. According to the legend, Wang was traveling through the Ch'en village when he saw some of the villagers boxing; unimpressed by their style, he made several disparaging remarks that naturally provoked them. They challenged him to a fight, and he defeated them soundly in little time. Awed by his great skill, the Ch'en family begged him to teach them his art, t'ai chi.[32] The first style of t'ai chi is named after the Ch'en family.

The Ch'en family continued to practice t'ai chi, but they kept it a secret from everyone outside of the village. Yang Lu-shan was the first person outside of the Ch'en family to learn t'ai chi from them, and he subsequently developed his own style of t'ai chi, later called the Yang style. Yang was a committed student of the martial arts, particularly Shao Lin boxing, but he was dissatisfied with that style. Having heard of a secret style of boxing in the Ch'en village, he sought out the family for instruction but was denied because he was not a member of the family. Yang decided to stay in the village, working as a servant with the hopes of learning the secret martial art. One night, he was awakened by noises in the courtyard; through a hole in the wall, he observed the Ch'en family practicing their t'ai chi. He continued to copy their form from his vantage point through the hole in the wall until he was finally caught and brought before Ch'en Chang Hsiang, the elder of the Ch'en clan. Before banishing him from the village, Ch'en Chang Hsiang asked Yang to demonstrate what he had learned of their form. The elder Ch'en was so impressed that he allowed Yang to continue studying the Ch'en style t'ai chi.[33]

Yang Lu-shan completely transformed the nature of t'ai chi practiced in China, due in part to his own commitment to the martial art and in part to the historical circumstances in China during the nineteenth and early twentieth centuries. Devoted to furthering the art of t'ai chi, Yang left the Ch'en village and traveled to Peking, where he was one of the first martial arts masters to teach openly. From Peking, t'ai chi spread throughout China. At the same time, China was colonized by the Japanese and by Europeans. In the face of colonization and the subsequent threats, both real and perceived, to many cultural traditions, Chinese martial arts began to be practiced more openly. They were upheld as examples of a distinctly national tradition, sources of pride and collective identity. The acts of warfare that brought the Japanese and Europeans into power in China, however, also made clear the emergence of new military technologies that quickly rendered the traditional martial arts obsolete. The inability of the traditional martial arts to withstand the new technologies of war proved tragic during the Boxer Rebellion when many Chinese fighters ran directly into enemy fire, believing that they would be safe from the bullets.[34]

The Chinese nationalist movement of 1912 ushered in new social structures as well as new attitudes toward technology and modernity.

To meet the new social demands, the Yang family adjusted its style of t'ai chi to emphasize "health, physical fitness, and techniques of self-defense." The Yang style departs sharply from its predecessor, the Ch'en style, which is characterized by "daring and dynamic movements, with changes of pace, of incredible, explosive energy, powerful kicks and punches, jumps and even a fall to the floor, where the Ch'en stylist does the splits." In contrast to the explosive, powerful style of the Ch'en family, the Yang style of t'ai chi emphasizes smooth, soft movements. By introducing moves that were accessible to most people, the Yang family made t'ai chi available to mass audiences. In addition, Yang broke the traditional secrecy of the martial arts master and promoted t'ai chi through the rhetoric of patriotism: "We are poor because we are weak; truly weakness is the cause of poverty. . . . The virility and vigor of the Europeans and Americans goes without saying. . . . From my youth I have always considered helping the weak as my personal responsibility. I have seen popular martial arts performers whose spirit and physique are in no way inferior to the so-called muscle men of the West."[35] Here, Yang upholds an exaggerated image of the West consistent with the imperialist rhetoric of the time, but he then uses it to extol the nationalist virtues of t'ai chi, which he believed could save the nation by strengthening the weak. Thus, largely through Yang's stylistic innovations and his nationalist rhetoric, t'ai chi flourished as a popular exercise throughout China.

T'ai chi was further institutionalized after World War II and the Communist Revolution as the Chinese sought to create a martial arts program that could be taught in schools and colleges. Toward this end, a number of famous teachers came together with athletic educators to produce the Wushu training system that emphasized athletic ability but without many of the older, more martial, combative techniques. Li Tian-ji, one of the collaborators and creators of the Wushu form, designed what is now known as the Combined Form, a long sequence that joins movements from different styles of t'ai chi, including both Yang and Ch'en. It was through the Combined Form that t'ai chi became widely popular, not so much in China as in the United States where Bow Sim Mark, a contemporary of Li Tian-ji's, introduced the form after emigrating and then publishing a book on the form in the late 1960s.[36]

Like yoga, t'ai chi is also rooted in a long tradition of philosophy and religion. Yet unlike many of the other martial arts systems which have at their foundations the principles of yin and yang, techniques of meditation, and even methods of controlling the ch'i (life force), t'ai chi relies heavily on the Taoist belief that the weak can prevail over the strong through softness and yielding. What Lao Tzu wrote in the *Tao Te Ching* (*Classic of the Way and the Power*) has been translated into practice in the art of t'ai chi: "Under heaven nothing is more soft and yielding than water. / Yet for attacking the solid and strong, nothing is better. / It has no equal. / The weak can overcome the strong; / The supple can overcome the stiff."[37] What separates t'ai chi from other martial arts is the emphasis on yielding to stronger forces as a means of eventually overpowering them. In this sense, it is literally an embodiment of Taoist philosophy.

According to the *Tao Te Ching*, the Tao—loosely defined as the infinite creative force—guides a person's life, and his or her Te—loosely defined as a person's power and natural strength—keeps him or her in alignment with the world.[38] People guided by the Tao and aligned by their Te enjoy simple, uncomplicated lives in harmony with nature. Those who achieve the highest levels in their t'ai chi practice can merge with the Tao, the eternal source of all things.[39] When Tao and Te are lost, "people perish because they have lost contact with their root." Again, t'ai chi translates Taoist philosophy into physical practice by drawing attention to the individual's sense of a physical root. Practitioners of t'ai chi first learn to keep their balance by standing and moving in ways that position the lower abdomen where the body's center of gravity should be.[40] At the same time, they also shift their consciousness from their minds to the lower abdomen and legs, a move which encourages a sense of rootedness. The ultimate goal is to transfer the sense of rootedness from a physical sensation to a mental and spiritual one.

A related tenet of Taoism is the emphasis on respecting what is natural and innate. Chuang Tzu, an early Taoist and author of *The Happy Journey or Excursion*, describes the potentially damaging and frequently violent effects of altering what is natural and innate. For instance, he gives the examples of trying to shorten a crane's legs, which can be done only by cutting them off, and trying to lengthen a duck's, which can only be done by painful stretching. In a less violent example, he describes a horse's natural condition and its unnatural condition in which it wears a saddle and bridle. From these examples, Chuang warns that any alteration of the natural and innate must be done very cautiously. In translating this idea to the physical practice of t'ai chi, practitioners work to understand what is natural and innate in their movements. While Paul Crompton acknowledges the fact that t'ai chi movements are not exactly natural to humans, he continues in somewhat circular fashion to suggest that the general movements of "civilized" people are even further removed from the natural and innate movements of humans; according to his reasoning, t'ai chi movements represent a return to a more natural and innate sense of movement. As with the principles of Tao, Te, and rootedness, practitioners of t'ai chi begin with the physical and aspire to the spiritual. That is, they begin by trying to become conscious of what is natural in their own motions and their body's way of practicing the various movements; from there, they strive to gain awareness not only of their physical movements but of their opinions, perceptions, and ideas as well until they eventually see the natural plurality of positions and pass through a state of enlightenment.[41]

Practitioners of t'ai chi also draw connections between t'ai chi and the concept of the five elements, the I-Ching, and the principles of yin and yang.[42] According to Chinese mythology, when the universe was created, everything divided into five elements—wood, earth, metal, fire, and water.[43] The five elements are remarkable in that they give rise to each other and are simultaneously capable of destroying each other, thus accounting for dynamic change in the universe. For instance, wood creates fire, fire creates earth (from ashes), earth creates metal, metal creates water (by attracting condensation), and water creates wood; in similar yet inverse fashion, fire burns wood and water quenches fire. The concept of the five elements was applied broadly to explain changes in both nature and society. Some practitioners of t'ai chi emphasized the connections between the various elements and types of t'ai chi movements. Thus, advances corresponded to metal, retreats corresponded to wood, looking left to water, looking right to fire, and being balanced corresponded to earth.[44] The possible relationships between two given elements provided a general orientation for the relationships between different movements; for example, a movement corresponding to water would overcome a technique corresponding to fire.

The constant change implicit in the concept of the five elements is further elaborated in the I-Ching and the principle of yin and yang which describes the opposite forces of the universe, forces that apply to everything in the universe. The fact that everything can be characterized by yin and yang led to a system of divination—the I-Ching—that relies on the predominance of yin or yang as represented by sixty-four hexagrams to help the diviner determine a response to the question at hand. Practitioners of t'ai chi have related the hexagrams to the physical t'ai chi movements, and along with the correlation of movements to the five elements, have come up with a suitably complicated and obscure system. A much more common application of yin and yang exists in the symbol that has come to be equated with yin and yang as well as with t'ai chi. Created in the eleventh century C.E. by the religious Taoist Chou Tun-yi to represent pictorially how immortality could be achieved, the Supreme Ultimate (commonly called the yin-yang) indicates the complete interrelationship of yin and yang. The symbol illustrates the two essential principles of yin and yang: (1) nothing is completely yin or yang, and (2) as one force increases, the other decreases. Practitioners of t'ai chi invoke this symbol because it so clearly illustrates the way in which aggression is diminished by yielding while yielding also has its limits. The relationship of t'ai chi to the principles of yin and yang extends far beyond the symbolic, however. Many see in the t'ai chi sequence a physical expression and interpretation of the yin and yang forces: "The positions of the palms, upward facing or downward facing, can be so interpreted, as can the fullness, weight bearing, or emptiness, non-weight bearing, of the feet. Breathing in and breathing out can be seen in the same way."[45] Here, the constantly changing movements within the sequence capture in physical motion the various philosophical concepts at the foundation of t'ai chi.

Yoga and T'ai Chi: From Philosophy to Physicality

Yoga and t'ai chi share similar legacies uniting philosophy, religion, and bodily practice, and both have come to represent long-standing Eastern traditions of holistic living. Yet their histories of migration, appropriation, and eventual establishment in the United States differ substantially. As mentioned above, yoga's fairly early presence in the United States arises out of active Hindu missionary work, particularly the work of Vivekananda and the Vedānta Society during the late nineteenth and early twentieth centuries. But even before Vivekananda's arrival, many Western scholars, philosophers, and poets were fascinated by Sanskrit texts and Indian philosophy and religion.[46] It was through these interests that they sought the origins of an Indo-European language as well as the key to life's mysterious, transcendental truths.[47] The colonial encounter introduced Indian culture, philosophy, and religion to the Western world on a popular level; what ensued was an orientalist fascination with the exotic, a fixation made familiar in the United States largely through the Transcendentalist writings of Emerson and Thoreau.[48] From the early nineteenth century on, many society men, and many more society women, were involved with social movements inspired by Indian religion and philosophy—Transcendentalism, Christian Science, Theosophy.[49] In familiarizing Indian philosophy while retaining enough of its exotic appeal, these social movements opened up a space in which yoga would later flourish.

On the other side of the colonial encounter, it seems that a growing nationalist response to British rule in India may have inspired a renaissance in the yogic traditions. Photographs taken in 1941 show Iyengar demonstrating different yoga poses in front of giant maps of India to reinforce the point that India was the origin of yoga.[50] Only a decade or so earlier, a small group of Indian scholars and yogis sought out the early yoga teachings and attempted to teach them to widespread secular audiences. That outside rule may have motivated a renewed interest in yoga as a consciously traditional, national practice coheres with other instances in which "folk traditions" were used to drive nationalist movements.[51] As previously discussed, colonial rule in China also inspired nationalist rhetoric concerning t'ai chi as well as broad-based exercise programs based on t'ai chi sequences. Of course, the colonial situations in India and China were drastically different, particularly with respect to the extent of Western involvement.

T'ai chi may be a much newer option in the global mall of alternative strategies for holistic living, but the trajectory of popular interest in it essentially replicates the trajectory of popular interest in yoga after Iyengar. In general, when people talk about yoga and t'ai chi today, they are referring to weekly, possibly semiweekly exercise classes presented with only a lasting trace of the philosophies at the heart of each system. Yet the overwhelming appeal of the trace philosophies—and the implicit promises of transformation through mind-body integration—accounts for the enormous surge in popular interest and continues to attract people to the practices.

The conceptual link between yoga and t'ai chi emerges from their ability to satisfy the same demand for self-consciously holistic physical exercise which is then reinforced through systems of commodification. For instance, the Living Arts catalogue offers yoga clothing, props, and instructional videos and books alongside t'ai chi (also marketed as Tao) shoes, clothes, instructional videos and books, jewelry, and general aids to meditation (cushions, music, incense). This link between yoga and t'ai chi is then completely naturalized through the design and discourse of the Living Arts catalogue which gives tangible form to the perception of a global mall of alternative strategies for holistic living. Recreation departments and health clubs, popular newspaper and magazine articles, and television and radio shows all do similar work to naturalize and maintain the imagined relationship between the two. Thus, as popularized in the United States, yoga and t'ai chi tend to sell the philosophical while practicing the physical, thereby largely separating the two practices from their respective belief systems that rely on physical movements as only one aspect of a complete practice.

Natural Fascinations and Fantasies

Consistent with other traditionalized bodily practices and various holistic approaches to living, yoga and t'ai chi are situated within the rhetoric of "the natural," rhetoric which participates in the broader risk society discourse by critiquing modernity through romanticized understandings of "other" people's connection to nature and "other" people's "intuitive" ability to live holistically. Thus, just as advocates of macrobiotic eating contrast "modern" and "traditional" diets to celebrate the imagined simplicity and purity of life prior to "today," proponents of yoga and t'ai chi often contrast "modern" and "traditional" exercise regimens to similar ends.

A common theme among advocates of yoga and t'ai chi is the argument that the two exercise programs deliver all the benefits of more intensely aerobic exercise without the impact, jarring motions, and tightness that exercises like running and aerobics inflict upon the body.[52] In this way, yoga and t'ai chi are coded as traditional health secrets and celebrated for accomplishing safely what modern exercise programs do but with risk to the body. A similar rejection of modern exercise exists in the contention that yoga exercises the body as fully as any machines or weight sets. For instance, Brian Vezina, a fitness expert, suggests that machines are passé: "You don't need weights and machines to work out. . . . There is a shift away from machines—that was so Eighties."[53] In many ways, the current nostalgia for an ancient, more "pure" past is a direct reaction to the egoism of the 1980s, which altered vast sectors of society (making some members obscenely wealthy and more incredibly impoverished) while also wreaking havoc on the environment. The 1980s witnessed phenomenal business freedoms, often with respect to environmental regulations, and in many cases, it is these very freedoms and technological advances that instigated risk society behaviors and beliefs. Thus, in associating machine-based workouts with the 1980s, Vezina is making a much broader statement about the superfluity—even danger—of technology, particularly as it relates to nature and health. To address these concerns, he has created an outdoor "boot camp" workout regimen to replace indoor health clubs and all of their machines. He ends his Central Park "boot camp" workouts with yoga and meditation as the sun sets over New York City. Another yoga instructor claims that "if you're ever stranded on a deserted island, you don't need anything else to stay in shape," as if staying in shape would be your biggest worry.[54] In keeping with a more natural orientation to living, yoga dismisses the need for technologically assisted exercise and foregrounds the artifice of running, walking, stepping, and biking without going anywhere.

At the same time, yoga and t'ai chi are also presented within the context of holism—a workout for the body, the mind, the soul. Implicit—and sometimes explicit—in such rhetoric is the contention that yoga and t'ai chi can help restore an individual's connections with nature, connections unfortunately ripped asunder by modern life. Both yoga and t'ai chi are said to be human reflections of the natural world and of natural phenomena. Along these lines, many of the yoga poses and t'ai chi movements are imitations of animals and animal behaviors. On more metaphorical levels, both traditions draw on the natural world to set standards for bodily practice. For instance, the qualities of water are also those that yogis strive to achieve: "Water has no shape of its own. It seems to have no strength, yet it can wear down rock over time. Water is constantly changing: ocean tides are pulled by the moon, rivers rise and fall with the seasons, the color of water changes depending on what is suspended in or reflected in it. . . . In yoga the qualities of water are often imitated. Like water, a Yogi strives to be able to change course 'on a dime,' ready for any new experience or thought beyond what is expected or imagined."[55] Thus, the imitation of water takes on holistic qualities; not only do yogis strive to make their bodies like water, but they also work to mimic the spirit of water through their attitudes and mental outlook.

Similarly, in t'ai chi, practitioners liken the fundamental concept of rootedness to the relationship between trees and the earth such that the metaphor is eventually literalized and t'ai chi becomes a practice through which the individual can experience deep connections with the earth: "In T'ai Chi a common image of rootedness is that of a tree whose roots descend deep into the earth's soil. This image extends to the practitioner who 'sinks into the ground' with invisible roots, so that, after many years of practice, he or she can actually feel as though they were connected deeply in and with the earth."[56] Here, metaphor and mimesis are powerful tools for effecting new perceptions of one's relationship to nature.

Through commodification and popularization, bodily and emotional imitations of nature quickly become yoga's and t'ai chi's interconnectedness with the natural world. The logic behind such a transference may be unclear, but the rhetoric is not. Such a romanticized association between yoga and t'ai chi and "nature" provides a sharp contrast to the ills of modernity, diseases which the two practices help address on individual levels: "As more and more of the people in our times have moved into the cities, grown up and been educated in the cities, this contact with the natural world has become very weak and sporadic. We do call for 'green' reforms, for a reduction in pollution and so forth, but the basis for our concerns is information fed to us by the media. We do not live in the countryside; we do not experience it directly. So if a rurally based society offers us something which has a 'natural' origin, we should grasp it with both hands, and feet, as it contains more than a whiff of clean air and a very stabilizing tempo."[57] This passage typifies the way in which t'ai chi is frequently positioned as a natural and intuitive response to the disturbing realities of the contemporary world. Not only have we lost our connection with nature by moving into cities, but we have also polluted and exploited the earth. In addition, our dependence on technologies like "the media" have only further exacerbated the cleavage between "society" and "nature." This idea recalls Tisserand's similar contention that it is the very symbols of modernity—telephones, computers, televisions—that prove destructive by spreading "war, political bias, and economic disaster."[58] Both Tisserand's aromatherapy and Crompton's t'ai chi begin to heal the damaging effects of modernity by reviving lost connections with nature. T'ai chi, offered up by the largely fictive rural society of China, benefits both the individual (through greater stability) and the global society (through metaphorical clean air).

The romanticization of nature and the imagined relationship between a traditionalized China and the natural world only essentializes and distances China from the perspective of the contemporary United States, an ideological move wholly consistent with the similar discourses of aromatherapy and macrobiotic eating. To suggest that people in China have not moved—and do not continue to move—to cities is absurd, especially given the fact that China has some of the world's most heavily populated cities. Even more, such a contrast between a "rurally based society" (i.e., China) and the modern United States freezes China in a pre-technological era without modern media technologies and industry to supplant more immediate experiences of "the countryside."

This idealization and essentialization of a pre-modern China enamored of nature is a common feature running throughout the t'ai chi discourse. For instance, one t'ai chi teacher compares Chinese and Western painting (as if the history of either had only one painting tradition) to demonstrate the way in which each culture perceives the relationship between people and nature. She contends that Chinese painters created immense landscapes with "huge mountains and vast skies" and tiny people whereas Western painters centered "man, large, at the center of the canvas" with nature receding into the background. Moreover, she interprets the globes, maps, calipers, and telescopes depicted in Western art as symbols of man's fascination with his ability to control nature; by contrast, the Chinese "with their reverence for nature, sought to merge themselves with it—to conform to the great reality."[59] Again, the simplification of East versus West romanticizes Chinese culture, removing it from the contemporary systems of global exchange and politics of which it is most definitely a part. Drawing a contrast between the nature-loving Chinese and the nature-controlling Westerners makes no sense as China prepares to build the world's largest dam, displacing 1.2 million people and wiping out nearly 7,000 villages, towns, and cities in the process of trying to control one of nature's most unforgiving powers.[60] Yet it is precisely this orientalist framework which continually draws people to t'ai chi and yoga; it is precisely this promise of an alternative exercise program grounded in ancient tradition and nature that sustains the commodification and the popularity of the two practices in the United States.

That the ideology of the alternative and the romanticization of the natural can have such appeal is explained in part by what ecopsychologists see as a general reorientation toward the earth and nature as sources of personal fulfillment. One prominent ecopsychologist contends that the disjuncture between people and nature is increasing and that people are becoming more conscious of—and hence alarmed by—such a breach. At the same time, a number of psychological studies suggest a link between spending time in nature and positive mental health. The practical applications of such findings are immense and, not surprisingly, often draw on bodily practices like yoga and t'ai chi to help people (re)establish what they perceive as lost connections with the earth and the natural environment. For instance, one psychologist has created a company called Earth Walk Adventures that combines "hiking and nature appreciation with such stress-reduction techniques as meditation, yoga and massage."[61] Through packaged and commodified experiences such as these, the association between yoga and "nature" is reinforced and further naturalized. No one seems surprised to find yoga on the agenda of Earth Walk Adventures' outdoor, back-to-nature activities.

The importance of the perceived and perpetuated relationship between yoga and t'ai chi and the natural environment and natural phenomena manifests itself—whenever possible—in the social space where yoga and t'ai chi are practiced. Thus, yoga studios, particularly the new franchised ones developed to meet the increasing demand for yoga classes in metropolitan areas, are described as "stylish, airy yoga centers,"[62] and words like "light" and "open" frequently accompany any descriptions of spaces designed particularly for yoga practice. Moreover, yoga ashrams and retreat centers are almost all located in remote wooded areas or on expansive beachfront sites. T'ai chi, even more than yoga, creates practice space close to nature, and in many cases, t'ai chi classes are held outside in parks: "Personally one of the happiest moments in T'ai Chi is when winter is over, and we can move our classes outside to a park. Our T'ai Chi takes on a new character as it resonates to the rhythms of spring. In contrast, one of the most difficult moments is when the weather grows inclement and we must return indoors. Yet even in the studio, closed off from the immediacy of nature, each time we begin the form, a memory is engaged that summons the summer stirrings of my inner self."[63] Here, the boundaries between indoor and outdoor space are blurred as the individuals in the class invoke their memories of practicing outside, closer to nature. Through such associations, memories, and even imaginings, the physical spaces in which t'ai chi and yoga are practiced open up into places of nature, thereby furthering the implicit (and sometimes explicit) association between the natural environment and these two bodily practices.

From Hatha to Eternity: Yoga in Paradise

The associations between t'ai chi and yoga and the natural environment are perhaps best articulated in the discourse of yoga retreats. Yoga retreats transfer the everyday social space of the yoga studio to one of two general sites—either serene, wooded forests or lush, tropical islands—where people can reestablish lost connections with the natural world. For instance, the Maple Ki Forest and Spirit Waters Yoga Retreat describes its surroundings by infusing nature with a magical, mystical quality: "Outdoors nature awaits with her own special gifts. Breathe deeply—the air is so fresh and sweet. The emerald waters of Bass Lake are pure and soft. Swimming is excellent. You may glide around the lake in a canoe or paddle boat and be gifted by sightings of resident wildlife and the haunting call of the loons."[64] Here, both nature and wildlife are personified in ways that emphasize the stereotyped association between nature and women. In this example, nature is clearly articulated as female, awaiting the visitor with "her" special gifts. She is "fresh and sweet" and "pure and soft" and even somewhat "haunting" as she draws people closer, away from civilization, modernity, technology.

There may be an initial danger in the lure of nature, but it is one which is thoroughly supported and easily overcome at Maple Ki. After all, reestablishing lost connections with nature cannot be too simple lest such retreats lose their drawing power, and Maple Ki positions itself as the perfect intermediary between "nature" and "society": "Do you long for something more than relief from the stresses and pressures of daily life? Time spent at Maple Ki is more. 'It is truly magical . . . a rare opportunity' . . . Maple Ki welcomes and supports you, not just 'getting away,' but 'coming home' in a most profound sense."[65] Again, Maple Ki supports the potentially difficult transition from "society" to "nature" and opens up a wide range of possibilities for reviving lost connections with nature, hence the idea of "coming home."

The Awakening in Paradise Yoga Retreat is the tropical complement to Maple Ki's wooded haven, and like Maple Ki, its promotional literature also opens by emphasizing the nurturing and magical qualities of nature: "Aloha! Join me on a nurturing and magical retreat in paradise at Mana Le'a Gardens, 'a Refuge from the Ordinary,' near Haiku on the beautiful island of Maui." Similarly, the Nosara Yoga Retreat in Costa Rica stresses the fact that it is literally situated within a natural wildlife preserve and within view of the Pacific Ocean: "Perched on a knoll overlooking the white sandy beaches of the Pacific, the Nosara Retreat is surrounded by a natural wildlife preserve. The diversity of animals and plants is unsurpassed. Catch glimpses of exotic, colorful birds or watch the fascinating antics of the howler monkey."[66] In the island paradise versions of the yoga retreat, the locale is made much more exotic than in the more familiar settings of the wooded forests, and it is through such exoticism that yoga practice is fully removed from the everyday. In general, the exotic surroundings of a tropical island and the sheer escapism of vacation are constructed to be relaxing in and of themselves. By situating yoga practice within such an environment, the discourse of yoga as a means of relaxation, healing, and stress release benefits from the participants' lived experience. Layered on top of the tropical surroundings and a yoga practice removed from the confines of everyday living are a wealth of other ways to relax—pre-arranged prepared meals, cleaning services, hot tubs, saunas, nature walks, massages, and bodywork. It is not surprising that such commodified and packaged experiences—built around yoga practice—are relaxing and rejuvenating. But perhaps the greatest beneficiaries of such effects are those who perpetuate, for whatever reasons, the discourse which unites yoga, nature, and mental and physical health (often through the idea of body-mind holism). In this way, yoga retreats continually infuse the broader yoga discourse with testimonials that bolster the belief in the more mundane, everyday practice and its relationship to the yoga-nature-holistic health paradigm for wellness.

While centers and programs like Maple Ki, Nosara, and Awakening in Paradise are all yoga retreats, the emphasis on yoga seems to recede into the background. As yoga practices are transferred from the everyday social space of the yoga studio to wooded retreats and tropical islands, the typically implicit associations between yoga and the natural environment are naturalized, thus bypassing any need to make them explicit. Outside of gyms—in "the natural environment"—yoga practitioners can easily imagine their reintegration with nature. One travel writer and participant of the Sivananda Ashram Yoga Retreat on Paradise Island in the Bahamas describes such an experience: "The first and last order of every day was a two-hour yoga class conducted on a platform that jutted out over the ocean. In these surroundings, yoga started to make more sense to me than it ever had in the power-yoga classes set to pounding music at my New York City gym. . . . I'll never forget the feeling of holding the Sun Salutation position as my classmates and I watched the first morning light spread over the ocean."[67] Here, the contrast between city gym and "natural" space also foregrounds an implicit contrast between modernity—as marked by New York City, the gym, the pounding music, even the concept of power yoga—and anti-modernity, characterized by the simple lifestyle of Sivananda—the family-style vegetarian meals at communal picnic tables, the shared clean-up, the sleeping bag accommodations, even the bugs. The idea of removing one's yoga practice to an environment like Sivananda,

Maple Ki, or Nosara does not seem at all odd, and it is precisely through such spatial transformations that yoga is coded as "natural," a coding further enhanced by the fact that very few hours of these yoga retreats are actually devoted to practicing yoga.

In this way, the conceptual associations between yoga and the natural environment as well as the associations between yoga and personal health are further enmeshed with risk society discourse. Because both yoga and t'ai chi are imagined to be deeply connected to nature—and thus rendered as such in commodified practice—they are also positioned as ways of contributing to the healing and protection of the environment and to the sustainable use of the earth's resources. The logic that relates these bodily practices to the health of the planet may not be especially clear, but the discourse is. For instance, one t'ai chi teacher quickly moves from the physical rootedness at the core of the t'ai chi technique to a metaphorical rootedness which individualizes the protection of the planet's resources: "On the deepest level, one's root is not merely a physical connection to the earth that is advantageous for push-hands, or one's health. Rather, it is a metaphor for becoming one with mother earth and her offspring, so that the destruction of nature's forests, for example, is literally a violation of one's own spiritual and physical being."[68] This same individualization of environmental protection and reverence for nature also surfaces in the yoga retreat discourse. Implicit in the promotional material for these retreats is a respect for the environment that suggests the type of spiritual ecological protection and activism described in the last quotation. At the same time, personal health is translated into planetary health such that the yoga-nature-health paradigm applies to individuals, to society, and to the planet: "They [the Nosara Retreat directors] will renew your joy for life and leave you feeling at peace with yourself, your family, your work and your world."[69] In essence, yoga retreats seem to promise a way of addressing the literal and metaphorical "violation of one's own spiritual and physical being" through individual nature appreciation.

The fact that yoga recedes into the background at most of these yoga retreats does not mean that the days are not full of organized activity. Most retreats offer a mélange of transcultural practices and rituals that imparts to the participants a certain multicultural spirituality. Thus, the Awakening in Paradise retreat in Maui, Hawaii, includes a soak in "2,000 year-old Birthing Pools," "a sacred sweat lodge ceremony, an introduction to body-mind connection through Syntropy," "massage and bodywork, lomi lomi [Hawaiian massage], acupuncture, [and] watsu." In similar fashion, the Yoga and Inner Vision Week annual healing retreat in Kauai, Hawaii, includes massage (Swedish, shiatsu, cranial sacral, deep tissue, and lomi lomi) as well as "acupressure, facials, aromatherapy, tai chi, chi gong, chiropractic adjustment and acupuncture [and] astrology and spiritual counseling."[70] In making accessible this wide array of transcultural "alternative" options for holistic life-enhancement, yoga retreats generate a sense of individual responsibility for personal, societal, and planetary health. Participants are forced into an immediate, often cultivated, intimacy with anywhere from five to fifty others, an environment in which the individual simultaneously works on self-improvement through the range of available bodily practices, on community building through the shared retreat experiences and rituals, and on planetary health through an appreciation and connection with the natural environment.

Yoga, T'ai Chi, and the Shape of a Woman

The discourse of personal responsibility associated with these alternative health practices is primarily a gendered one, especially when it appeals to self-improvement and bodily transformation. Like aromatherapy, yoga and t'ai chi are positioned as means by which women can control their beauty, their health, and ultimately their sex appeal and happiness. The rhetoric of women's magazines is transferred not only to the packages and labels of aromatherapy products but also to the realm of women's sports and fitness through the fairly recent growth of magazines devoted to women and sports. Thus, the hegemonic ideals of women's magazines—the heterosexist ideologies which assume and advocate women's desire to live up to white, upper-middle-class standards of beauty and body shape to attract men—easily translate from women's magazines to aromatherapy packaging to macrobiotic cookbooks and magazines devoted to women and sports. That old ideologies are continually embellished with new—but empty—rhetorics of gender and social power attests to the depth and breadth of these cultural beliefs that offer a ready-made setting for beliefs and assumptions about yoga, t'ai chi, and the gendered aspects of bodily transformation.

Women's magazines, and the fashion and beauty industry to which they are tied, are notoriously slow to reflect social change and have changed little since the 1950s.[71] For the most part, the magazines still concern themselves with hair and make-up tips, fashion trends, diet and weight-loss advice, and suggestions for pleasuring men; as discussed in the previous chapters, the general tone of the articles and advertisements is one of control—control over all aspects of a woman's happiness from beauty and body to sex and relationships. The recent emergence of women's magazines devoted to sports and fitness may seem to alter some of the dominant ideological positions of the more traditional women's magazines by emphasizing women's participation in both professional and recreational sports, many of which are typically associated with men. The tone of these women's sports and fitness magazines is one of power and strength, the post-1970s feminist rhetoric with an athletic, sporting theme. Despite the new rhetoric, however, the old ideologies and equations persist as fashion articles simply feature the most figure-flattering workout and sports clothes, beauty articles range from skin treatments to lip exfoliation for "athletic" women, articles about men still fit virtually any category, and the diet and weight-loss features are hardly transformed at all, ranging from "success stories" to explicit day-by-day diets to specific exercises for particular body parts.

From the sheer volume of articles on bodies, body parts, diets, eating (or not eating), and "success stories," the underlying message of these sports and fitness magazines has to do with transforming women's bodies—often quickly, easily, and cheaply—both to please one's self and to please others. Thus, as one journalist notes, the take-charge, powerful tenor of women's sports and fitness magazines simply repackages traditional women's magazines in a slightly different way: "All of which suggests that even in the third decade of the women's movement—after women have ascended in fields like politics, business and publishing, and presumably have a wide range of interests—the magazines that serve them seem intent on remaining basically the same, as interested in recipes, diets, makeovers and blind dates as they were in the 1970's."[72] In addition to a new discursive strategy, women's sports and fitness magazines draw on alternative health, exercise, and fitness practices as a way of seeming new and innovative, and it is within this context that yoga and t'ai chi—as well as meditation, "ancient" Eastern breathing techniques, martial arts, and aromatherapy products—are presented as sports, as aids to better athletic performance, and most commonly as simple means to "better" bodies and thus better lives.

Within this sports and fitness as beauty and sexuality framework, yoga and t'ai chi are celebrated for their transformative potentials. As with all the exercise programs in these magazines, they seem to offer quick, easy ways of toning the body, and in some cases, they are even upheld for their stress-reducing qualities, a seemingly added benefit to the physical wonders that they work. Thus, a *Fit* magazine cover screams "Yoga for Hard, Tight Thighs" in an explicit appeal to external, physical bodily transformation. Here, yoga becomes yet another "quick route to perfection" designed to sell magazines.[73] In fact, thighs seem to be an especially popular area for yogic transformation. Another article promises "Less Inner Thigh, More Inner Peace" in a headline that seems to focus more on the spiritual side of yoga.[74] It doesn't take long for the article's real emphasis to emerge, however; first, then, the subtitle gives it all away: "Our yoga workout will give you lean, sexy legs and a shot of serenity, too. Om, sweet, Om!" Clearly, serenity and inner peace are secondary to "lean, sexy legs."

Similarly, an article on yoga as part of a series on spa living at home gives lip service to yoga as a practice for mind-body integration by opening with a quote from Dan Howard of Canyon Ranch in the Berkshire Mountains of Massachusetts; yet even in descriptions of yoga as a mind-body practice, its ability to transform the body comes to the fore: "The photographs here show three classic poses that illustrate yoga's versatility, from reshaping your body to rejuvenating your mind." With photographs of a tall, slender, white woman demonstrating the poses, the emphasis is clearly on the shape of a "beautiful body" as articulated in the description of the first pose: "Build a Strong, Beautiful Body. Yoga can make you lean and strong. And its emphasis on body alignment and stabilization of your body's core... translates to better posture."[75] Here, strength is equated with beauty, and yoga is a rather peaceful, simple way of building strength—and thus acquiring beauty—especially for women who might not like the cardiovascular challenges and sweat of more aerobic workouts. At the same time, the culturally valued "lean" body is the implied result of yoga practice, much as it was invoked as the result of living and eating according to macrobiotic principles. Women's sports and fitness magazines further idealize this body through photographs of models practicing the various yoga poses.

Not surprisingly, articles about yoga and t'ai chi in women's fashion magazines sound exactly like those in women's sports and fitness magazines. One such article also implies the relationship between yoga and t'ai chi and the "lean" body: "Fitness buffs have rejected the tight, chiseled Madonna look, achieved by intense weight and aerobic training in favor of a long, lean appearance."[76] Another article about "no-sweat fitness" opens by critiquing the 1980s-style workout while celebrating yoga and t'ai chi as ways of relieving stress in addition to transforming the body: "Remember '80s exercise? It was sweaty, loud and painful. We went for the burn, and many of us burned out. Now we're turning to the relaxing workout—one that slims and tones but also relieves stress."[77] And, like women's sports and fitness magazines, fashion magazines use photographs of tall, slender ("lean") white models doing yoga and t'ai chi—the supposed proof that yoga and t'ai chi really do deliver on the implicit promises to slim and tone.

While t'ai chi has not attained yoga's level of popularity, it also surfaces in all varieties of women's magazines as an alternative exercise for toning muscles, improving balance and coordination, and even teaching women to move more gracefully. And, unlike articles on yoga, the ones about t'ai chi often draw attention to the fact that t'ai chi is an exercise in mind-body integration as well as a physical exercise with the potential to transform the body. The different approaches to describing yoga and t'ai chi in women's magazines likely emerge out of the relative familiarity of yoga, in contrast to the relative exoticness of t'ai chi. Thus, yoga is frequently distanced from its mystical origins and New Age, aging hippie associations: "No longer perceived as mystical mumbo jumbo for new age neophytes, yoga is being embraced for its wide range of benefits" and "the new yoga devotees are not flaky, zonked-out hippies or macrobiotic New Agers."[78] Similarly, yoga studios and health clubs offering yoga classes are careful to find instructors who will play up yoga's physical benefits while downplaying the more philosophical, mystical aspects:

"Some yoga instructors have made their classes more mainstream simply by editing out the more spiritual aspects of yoga" and "health clubs, for example, are wary of putting their customers off with too much Eastern mysticism."[79] In many cases, innovative yoga instructors go further in making yoga familiar by setting it to music, making it intensely aerobic, combining yoga positions with dance moves, and creating classes which bring yoga together with more conventional strength training and stretching.

In contrast to both yoga discourse and yoga practice as described in women's magazines, t'ai chi is generally exoticized and "authenticated" by its adherence to the thirty-seven traditional moves of the Yang form, the style of t'ai chi most commonly practiced in the United States. In addition, the t'ai chi discourse tends to focus on how the practice stimulates internal energy to make people feel calmer, more centered, and generally happier after they have completed a t'ai chi session. For instance, instructors clearly articulate the relationship between t'ai chi and internal energy: "T'ai chi really emphasizes working from the inside out. It's about internal energy," and "the exercises leave you calm, yet alert and energized."[80] Although many popular yoga instructors and practitioners writing about their yoga experiences distance themselves from too much Eastern mysticism, they will nonetheless draw out Eastern ideas about the body's energy systems, particularly as they relate to nature and the universe: "[T'ai chi] is sometimes described as an internal martial art, although in this case that's because a practitioner's skill in doing it depends on her ability to control subtle energy flows within the body. The slow, fluid movements, based on forces in nature, supposedly open the body's energy gates and allow chi from nature and the universe to enter its major pathways."[81] Despite the writer's slight skepticism, t'ai chi is clearly identified as a non-Western, somewhat mystical form of exercise, one ultimately capable of directing the body's energy and transforming the shape of a woman's body. Along these lines, one writer claims, "You'll see better muscle tone in two to three months. . . . Eventually the practitioner is supposed to become aware of the Chi, or energy, coursing through her body and be able to mentally focus it."[82]

In the end, women's magazines orchestrate the familiar versions of yoga and the exotic discussions of t'ai chi around themes of control and personal responsibility—the hallmarks of women's magazines since their inception. According to these articles, practicing yoga encourages women to take control of their bodies and their beauty (albeit more gently than with aerobics), while t'ai chi exercises allow women to control their energy, their states of well-being, and the shape of their bodies. In this way, women's magazines translate their dominant ideologies of beauty, health, sexuality, and gender to yoga and t'ai chi exercises. The considerations of yoga and t'ai chi in women's magazines give a particularly gendered spin to the usual discourses in which these two bodily practices are immersed. Thus, reestablishing connections with the natural environment and setting aside the stresses of modern living blend with concerns about beauty, bodies, health, and sex appeal. As with the aromatherapy discourse on product labels and packaging, the articles about yoga and t'ai chi in women's magazines situate beauty, health, and sexuality within the broader contexts of individual, familial, social, even planetary responsibility, and once again women are summoned as everyone's caregivers. In essence, yoga and t'ai chi are good for inner peace, relaxation, stress reduction, and the shape of a woman's body, all of which are said to contribute to better self-esteem, better relationships, and thus a better society and a better world. One woman's yoga class makes explicit this sense of social responsibility: "We end the class by chanting for world peace."[83] From personal body "reshaping" to world peace, the yoga and t'ai chi discourses in women's magazines reiterate the fact that it is women who are to carry the burden of individual, familial, social, and planetary wellness.

Color Coded: The Semiotics of Commodified Practice

From the glossy pages of women's magazines to the celluloid strips of instructional videos, those practicing yoga and t'ai chi are noticeably white (though often tanned) and their bodies almost always adhere to Western cultural ideals—tall, long-legged, lean women and tall, muscular men. In many of the yoga videos featuring women, the instructors are often famous models, actresses, and fitness gurus with their own television shows—Jane Fonda, Ali McGraw, Dixie Carter, Kathy Smith, Denise Austin—and thus, it is not surprising that their bodies symbolize the ideal. Similarly, the men tend to be fitness gurus, martial arts specialists, or famous yoga instructors, and they frequently look like models in men's magazines like *GQ* and *Esquire*. As yoga and t'ai chi are commodified through such means as these instructional videos, the ethnic associations of the two practices are effaced, and idealized white bodies come to represent the two bodily practices. It is through this erasure and choreographed ethnomimesis that Western bodies are initially made foreign and then familiar in attempts to transform them into culturally valued forms.

One of the most popular yoga videos is the *Jane Fonda Yoga Workout*, which features the slender, slightly muscular woman whose body essentially represents the physically fit, and thus beautiful, standard. Here, Jane Fonda wears a wine-colored unitard which highlights her pale skin, especially in contrast to the odd cloudy gray set which is probably supposed to invoke some New Age association. Most noticeable, however, is her blonde hair, piled high and descending into a French braid that hangs to her waist. Aside from accentuating Jane Fonda's blondeness and whiteness, the braid (obviously a hair extension) does little but get in her way as she moves through the series of sun salutation poses. All of the other popular and widely accessible yoga videos feature white women whose bodies fit the culturally valued form. In some cases, their bodies even become criteria by which reviewers evaluate the tapes: "The tall and lean Smith [Kathy Smith, fitness tape maven] is appealing as a yoga instructor.... Her [Denise Austin, ESPN fitness specialist] perfectly shaped and toned muscles are appealing and well-suited for some of the positions and postures demanding strength."[84] With the popularity of other yoga videos by actresses like Ali McGraw and Dixie Carter (who has two tapes to her name), it is clear that white women and their "lean," "perfectly shaped" bodies have largely erased yoga's ethnic associations, at least through the "ideology of the image."[85]

In this way, yoga is made familiar for Western tastes. For the most part, the poses are not referred to by their Sanskrit names but by their English translations, and the emphasis on physicality over philosophy is abundantly clear. In promoting their videos, Fonda, McGraw, and Carter have all foregrounded yoga as their preferred way of keeping fit. For instance, Carter credits yoga with maintaining her physique: "In terms of staying in shape, as in getting into the size 6 and having a small waistline, yoga does it all. . . . My legs are prettier than they were then [at twenty-five], and I have a better figure because of yoga."[86] Though the video yoga instructors give lip service to breathing techniques, relaxation, and stress reduction, the priorities—both theirs and their viewers—lie with yoga's potential to transform their bodies into the cultural ideal. The belief in the ability of both yoga and t'ai chi to transform the physical shape of the body is most clearly articulated in *Buns of Steel Power Yoga* and *Buns of Steel T'ai Chi*. To present yoga poses and t'ai chi moves within the "of Steel" series highlights the most extreme degree to which the two bodily practices have been thoroughly commodified and re-moved from their cultural and philosophical contexts. Not surprisingly, the instructors in the *Buns of Steel Power Yoga* and *Buns of Steel T'ai Chi* videos are fit, muscular, and white.

Buns of Steel Power Yoga and *Buns of Steel T'ai Chi* also highlight the extremely lucrative nature of the relationship between these practices and their transformative potential as New Age exercise regimens. Howard Maier, the president and one of the owners of Yoga Zone (see Chapter 1), is also the marketing genius responsible for taking the "Buns of Steel" line of exercise videos to their current position on top of the market.

Consistent with the discourses about yoga and t'ai chi in women's magazines, t'ai chi videos are more ethnically marked than the yoga videos, though most of the instructors in popular and easily accessible videos are also white. Most of the t'ai chi instructors invoke the ethnic associations through their dress—baggy "t'ai chi" pants and long, loose, tunic-style shirts, often with Mandarin collars and fastened with Chinese "frogs" (complicated knot clasps). The most noticeable difference between the yoga videos and the t'ai chi videos is in the sex of the instructors. While yoga videos overwhelmingly feature women, the t'ai chi videos tend to feature men, probably due to the fact that the initial t'ai chi practitioners in this country were largely involved with the martial arts community, which was overwhelmingly male. Along these lines, one of the most popular t'ai chi videos features actor David Carradine, who starred in the television series *Kung Fu*. Here, Carradine has merged his television persona with a martial arts background to move t'ai chi further into the mainstream.

While yoga and t'ai chi videos tend to erase any trace of the nonwhite historical practitioners, they still invoke discourses of nature and rely on iconic representations of the Eastern cultures from which the practices originate. Thus, many videos are set outdoors, thereby visually summarizing all of the back-to-nature discourse surrounding these two practices. For instance, Ali McGraw's *Yoga: Mind and Body* is set in White Sands, New Mexico, where the white sand dunes contrast beautifully with the intensely blue sky in a cinematic articulation of the idea that yoga practice returns the practitioner to an exoticized, edenic paradise. In similar fashion, Denise Austin's *Yoga Essentials* is set in Utah's Zion National Park, a setting of red rock canyons and rock formations that reinforces the connection between yoga practice and the natural environment. A PBS series entitled *T'ai Chi in Paradise* is filmed outdoors in Hawaii, thus continuing the trend of removing both yoga and t'ai chi practice to wooded retreats or tropical islands. When filmed indoors, the videos subtly highlight icons of Eastern ethnicity so as to combine the westernization of the practitioners and the practices themselves with enough ethnic associations to maintain the lure of the exotic. Thus, for instance, the touches might be as small and understated as the "t'ai chi" clothes or the oriental carpet that Lilias Folan uses instead of a yoga mat in *Lilias! Yoga Workout.*

Ultimately, it is this duality and the replacement of racially coded bodies that enables the full commodification of yoga and t'ai chi. Through the visual cues and ideologies, yoga and t'ai chi videos make the body simultaneously foreign and familiar, highlighting the transformative potential of these two bodily practices. In essence, viewers have the voyeuristic opportunity to witness the physical ethnomimesis which occurs as Jane Fonda, Kathy Smith, Ali McGraw, and David Carradine put their bodies through the "foreign" yoga poses and t'ai chi moves. At the same time, however, viewers see—and are likely attracted to—the familiar ideals of fitness and beauty. As with macrobiotic eating and aromatherapy, the process of ethnomimesis is an exceptionally superficial one, though one with the promise and potential for permanent transformation as evidenced by the tall, slender, slightly muscular, slightly curvaceous bodies of the instructors.

Conclusion

Through the visual discourses of race, ethnicity, and gender implicit in cultural productions like popular magazines and instructional videos, commodified versions of yoga and t'ai chi foreground the transformative potential of both practices through a simultaneous exoticization and familiarization of the body. This very physical ethnomimesis invites both voyeuristic and bodily participation such that individuals can determine the extent to which they embody the ideologies of nature, multiculturalism, gender, health, and beauty implicit in the discourses surrounding these bodily practices. Positioned within larger discourses of nature, the environment, and risk society, the ideologies of the body conveyed through commodified versions of yoga and t'ai chi encourage personal responsibility for everything from individual health and beauty to planetary wellness. And, similar to the cases of aromatherapy and macrobiotic eating, it is mainly women who are presumed to be engaged with external bodily concerns that eventually blend with social and planetary concerns.

5

RISKS OF MODERNITY

Consumption as Political Action

In reading the complex and intersecting discursive fields of the three cases at the core of this study, I have grounded the everyday ideologies implicit in the commodified discourses of alternative health in an analysis that integrates a critique of the public sphere, the global marketplace, modernity, and the transformative potential of traditionalized and commodified bodily practices. Throughout, I have drawn on this model as a means of understanding the social and political relationship between public discourses of alternative health and the individualization of those discourse within the contexts of identity, ideology, and modernity.

The discourses surrounding the commodification of aromatherapy, macrobiotic eating, yoga, and t'ai chi all seek to confront the hegemony of science and technology implicit in the project of Western modernization. Thus, aromatherapy practices are upheld as alternatives to Western biomedicine, particularly drug therapies, and the products themselves are celebrated for the positive impact that their production has on the environment, contrasted sharply with the more deleterious effects of growing plants with pesticides and harvesting plant products without concern for long-term sustainability. Macrobiotic eating figures similarly in discourses of alternative health and living that foreground cultural critique; in emphasizing organic, unprocessed foods, the discourse of macrobiotic eating condemns the use of pesticides and processing, both of which lead to various forms of environmental pollution. Along the same lines, yoga and t'ai chi are offered as alternatives to the machine-based exercise technologies that remove us from the natural world, further fragmenting individual and environment.

This mode of cultural critique in popular discourses relies upon an Eastern agelessness, in opposition to a Western modernity. Without question, "Western" and "Eastern" are elaborate constructions, and such inventions only further the orientalist fantasies at their core. In this way, the West is represented as a highly individualized, technologized, and scientized modernity, while the East remains the timeless representation of collectivity, spirituality, nature, and harmony. It is precisely this imagined contrast that allows for cultural critique by creating "a position from which to reappraise and reform the institutions and thought systems indigenous to the west."[1] Here, Clarke refers largely to the way academics have understood and approached the East and Eastern systems of thought and belief in relation to Western reform. Within such a context, the complicated and enduring relationship between Eastern and Western systems of thought and belief may frequently open up spaces for sincere cultural critique. In the popular imagination, however, East and West are caricatured in ways that render any cultural critique meaningless. Rather than subvert the hegemony of the Western Enlightenment project, the discourses of these bodily practices reinforce it by invoking the impression of critique as a marketing device and a selling point.

For instance, in its lifestyle magazine the aromatherapy company Aveda poses a rhetorical question to remind consumers of the dangers of participating in modern society: "In today's fast-paced world, we often push ourselves to do it all—faster, better, and more completely. But what's the cost to physical and mental health?" Here, the use of Aveda's aromatherapy products—which are said to be premised on the principles of Ayurvedic medicine, "a complex science born in India 5000 years ago"—helps defray the "cost to physical and mental health" that results from modern living. In this value-laden contrast between Western modernity and India of five thousand years ago, Aveda gives the impression of participating in a cultural critique of modernity and of the technologies enabling "today's fast-paced world." Aveda's use and celebration of technological innovations like the bioactivity camera, however, typify the hollow nature of any rhetoric intended to critique the superiority of Western modernity: "Aveda also offers consumers new technology that helps demonstrate the efficacy of aroma on emotional states: bioactivity cameras. Available at select Aveda locations, these cameras capture impressions of the electrical field that surrounds people and represents their emotional and physical health." After all, it is the "new technology" that essentially proves the validity of aromatherapy and, implicitly, of Ayurvedic medicine. Through the bioactivity camera Aveda makes available for purchase the *idea* of participating in cultural critique, of living according to ancient philosophies, of living an alternative lifestyle. The irony of this type of East-West contrast is not unique to Aveda but characterizes the discourse surrounding all of the practices and products explored in this book.

Through commodification and consumption, seemingly subversive cultural critiques are integrated into systems of New Age capitalism. As demonstrated through the example of Aveda, any cultural critique is an ironic one as consumption becomes a mode of addressing social, political, and cultural disenchantment, although the very processes enabling consumption are what characterize modernity, itself the cause of the disenchantment being critiqued. This irony is paralleled, and to a certain extent anticipated, by Habermas in his critique of the transformation of the public sphere.[2] For Habermas, the bourgeois public sphere was made possible largely through the early processes of capitalism, yet it is the fully developed capitalist system that ultimately threatens the active participation and rational discourse necessary for democracy to thrive. Along these lines, the mediation of discourse—a core feature of commodity culture—transfers ideological convictions from the private realm (where Habermas contends they must remain) to a public sphere that *seems* to engage in rational-critical debate around the personalization of political issues. Yet, capitalism does more than contain active participation through communicative action; it authorizes the purchasing of participation. By purchasing the products of commodified bodily practice, and thereby "buying into" the discourses that constitute the public sphere of alternative health and wellness, individuals can lay claim to active political participation. By recycling the discourses inscribed on the surfaces of consumer culture—product packaging, print advertisements, and in-store displays—and through shared face-to-face communication, individuals can see themselves as engaging in the rational-critical discourse that seems to politicize the public sphere of alternative health and wellness.

The supposed rational-critical discourse of the public sphere of alternative health and wellness revolves around the primary themes of Ulrich Beck's risk society. The risks of modernity—which also motivate the popular orientalist attitude characteristic of the rhetoric of aromatherapy, macrobiotic eating, yoga, and t'ai chi—infuse the messages, beliefs, and assumptions surrounding these commodified bodily practices with a sense of political urgency, an urgency that appeals to personal, social, and planetary wellness. At the same time, Beck suggests that most techno-industrial societies are in transition between classic industrial societies, where the primary political concerns relate to class and equality issues, to risk societies, where the primary political concerns relate to individualization and protection from the dangers of a too successful modernity. Despite the fact that class societies and their attendant problems of equality have not vanished with the development of the welfare state and the increased dependence on technological advances, political and popular attention to these concerns has diminished with the transition to risk society and its emphasis on the individual. As Beck argues, "the hierarchical model of social classes and stratification has increasingly been subverted," as well as being depoliticized and essentially ignored.[3] Ultimately, the self becomes the site of political action. In a way that recalls nineteenth-century efforts to translate individual bodily concerns to the social body, this movement toward the self also renders the individual political.

In contrast to the nineteenth-century discourses which saw the body politic as an extension of the individual body, risk society discourse individualizes social illnesses in a way that isolates the individual body from the body politic, and "social crises appear as individual crises, which are no longer (or are only very indirectly) perceived in terms of their rootedness in the social realm."[4] The public sphere of alternative health and wellness plays upon this individualization of social risks. The popular discourses around the practices discussed in this study, as well as a wide range of other New Age practices and products, address precisely these individual manifestations of social disease. The care and nurturing of the self is broadly thematized and central to the successful transformation of these practices into products. At the same time, attempts to repair the disjuncture between the social nature of risk and the individualization of its effects can open up discursive spaces in which the impression of cultural critique, made possible through popular orientalism and risk society discourse, can flourish. The public sphere of alternative health and wellness sells the supposed means of addressing the individualization of social disease while also critiquing the necessity of dealing with the transfer of disease from the body politic to the individual body.

As discussed throughout this book, personal consumption becomes political action through participation in this public sphere of alternative health and wellness. Personal health is quickly translated into social and planetary wellness through aromatherapy's emphasis on stress reduction and natural plant essences, through macrobiotic eating's emphasis on organic foods and sustainable agriculture, through yoga's and t'ai chi's imagined connections with ancient spirituality and natural means of spreading peace and harmony. As Beck makes explicit, however, the radical individualism and political discourses of risk society—reinscribed in the consumer culture of the public sphere of alternative health and wellness—obscure the issues of power and inequality at the core of class society. While Beck does not imply that the political aspects of risk society discourses are some sort of capitalist diversionary tactic designed to bypass issues of class and equality, I would suggest that the way risk society concerns are presented and packaged as commodities in the public sphere of alternative health and wellness contributes to the displacement of class and equality concerns that are fundamental to any sincere form of social critique and social reform. Attention to class and equality issues is supplanted by concern for individual and planetary wellness, considerations that are easily accommodated through consumption as a mode of social action.

Through consumption as social and political action, individuals can enjoy the sense of primary engagement with rational-critical discourse in the public sphere of alternative health. Consumer choices become political choices as shoppers seek out the most "socially responsible" companies—the most environmentally conscious packaging, recycled materials, the nonaerosol sprays, organic foods, products that contribute to funds and organizations set up "for" indigenous cultures. The simultaneous consumption of both the messages and the products supposedly constitutes a political participation that appeases the conscience but essentially ignores the inadequacies and inequalities of Western welfare states. Individuals can thus personally work toward care of the society and care of the planet through care of the self.

Furthermore, this sort of participation is available to limited segments of society. Only those with the leisure time and disposable income for such luxury items and practices can exercise this peculiar type of political action through consumption. Despite discursive attempts to protect or remove these spiritual, bodily practices from systems of exchange and materiality, they remain deeply entrenched in capitalist systems of production and consumption. That healing practices like aromatherapy and macrobiotic eating and spiritual endeavors like yoga and t'ai chi are involved in systems of exchange is nothing new. In the imagined history of aromatherapy, for instance, individuals made offerings to the Greek gods in exchange for healing treatments. Similarly, individual study with a yogi often involved an exchange of household work on the initiate's part. What is new here is their commodification, the public discourses generated by such commodification, and the exclusionary nature of any capitalist exchange system.

Somewhat ironically, these bodily practices are at once status symbols and icons of a life outside of the American mainstream where material concerns reign supreme. Because of their associations with fantastic constructions like "nature" and the "East"—romantic ideals in contradistinction to Western capitalism—aromatherapy, macrobiotic eating, yoga, and t'ai chi are upheld in the public sphere of alternative health for the "authentic" experience associated with their practice, an experience believed to be lost with their commodification. At the same time, these bodily practices are often so expensive as to rank as status symbols while having the added cultural value of seeming to be anti-status and thus somehow more morally gratifying than 1980s-style ostentation. Kathleen A. Hughes of the *Wall Street Journal* catalogues some of the new, "more understated must-haves"—personal trainers, "power" yoga, personal chefs who can cook a seven-course vegetarian dinner, and interesting vacations such as treks through Nepal.[5] It is precisely because status symbols such as these fully embrace the ideology of alternative practices and places that they have become so popular, especially with aging baby boomers who are increasingly concerned with their own health, fitness, mortality, and thus spirituality. The imagined anti-status of these trends and other practices like the ones discussed in this book also implies a certain equal accessibility, the somewhat naive American belief that health, fitness, and spirituality are available to everyone. Thus, in this way too, participation in the public sphere of alternative health through the consumption of these bodily practices gives the impression of positive political action. Yet it is clear that the shift from ostensible status symbols to understated ones does nothing to redistribute wealth, nor to make health, wellness, and spirituality equally accessible. Consumption is obviously not political action, despite the popular New Age discourses aspiring to make it so.

Moreover, the language of consumption as political action is not contained within the public sphere of alternative health and wellness. Rather, it seeps out and into the consumer landscape through the advertisements for a wide range of goods and services, particularly luxury items and investment services. And yet, even when it is a car and not a yoga video that is for sale, an association with individual wellness and spirituality reiterates the logic of the public sphere of alternative health that upholds social and planetary wellness as side-effects of personal wellness. For instance, an advertisement for the Jeep Grand Cherokee, a large, four-wheel-drive off-road vehicle, draws an explicit—if somewhat tongue-in-cheek—relationship between the luxury vehicle and yoga. The advertisement's headline reads: "The Nine Principal Postures for Achieving Greater Relaxation and Self-Discovery." Surrounding the banner are silhouettes of eight yoga positions, with their English names beneath in parentheses; the ninth, and center, position is a silhouette of a man reclining as if behind the wheel of a car. The text in parentheses reads: "The Jeep Grand Cherokee." While the images and the ideas create the slightly humorous tone of the advertisement, the main body of the ad still takes the core ideas seriously: "Any journey of self-discovery starts by finding a quiet place. Inside a Jeep Grand Cherokee Limited, for example. With rich leather-trimmed seats, Automatic Temperature Control and the Jeep Memory System, relaxation is assured. Now picture a secluded location and prepare to unwind . . . Jeep ownership. It's a position that's easier than ever to get into." Here, as in the discourses of yoga, t'ai chi, macrobiotic eating, even aromatherapy, self-discovery is the initial point of action. Again, the turn toward the self, the individualization of society, is the first step in the personal healing which ultimately motivates social and planetary wellness.

Clearly, cars seem to rival all New Age practices as a means to self-discovery. A similar advertisement for the Chevy Tahoe, also a sport utility vehicle (and a very large one), takes a much more serious tone than the Jeep advertisement. A photograph of the Chevy Tahoe in the midst of a forest with hazy, almost ethereal sunlight shining through the trees is accompanied by text that is clearly secondary to the picture. The hardly noticeable quotation from Thoreau at the top of the page is a key to the photograph: "I never found the companion that was so companionable as solitude." Beneath the photograph, in even smaller type, the text claims: "Chevy Tahoe, the one sport utility vehicle whose vast size and comfort make it perfect for self-discovery." In keeping with the themes of self-discovery and nature at the core of the public sphere of alternative health, this advertisement suggests that purchase of the Chevy Tahoe not only enables self-discovery but also makes possible natural spaces such as the forest in the photograph. The height of the trees surrounding the Chevy Tahoe dwarfs its "vast size" and essentially naturalizes its presence in an otherwise isolated forest.

Sport utility vehicles capable of taking their drivers "off-road" and thus away from "civilization" are not the only automobiles capable of inspiring inner peace and self-discovery. One advertisement for a Toyota Corolla features a yin-yang pendant at the top of the page and, at the bottom, a photograph of the car in the middle of a large Japanese-style rock garden with designs combed in the sand. The headline claims: "proof that your heart and head can reach perfect harmony." Once again, the benefits of bodily practices like t'ai chi are transferred to the luxury products of modernity, and consumption becomes an easy and immediate way of attaining the desired spiritual results.

Even in cases like that of the Toyota Corolla—where consumption is for personal and not necessarily social and planetary wellness—the associations explicit in the advertisement fix the product in an entire system of consumption that eventually makes clear the purported interdependency of personal, social, and planetary health, thus reinforcing the odd logic of consumption as social and political action. For instance, the large companies that supply the gasoline that these automobiles need to move their owners toward enlightenment appeal to environmental concerns as primary selling points. An advertisement for Chevron gasoline describes a tidewater wetland that it created next to its refinery in Pascagoula, Mississippi. Chevron admits that it built this wetland as part of a deal that would allow the company to expand its refinery operations in the area, but it also details the ways in which it "surpassed requirements for the wetland both in design and acreage." Here, Chevron trades on its seeming generosity to suggest that the environment is more important than any financial considerations. In fact, the advertisement closes with such a claim: "Typically our technology is used to affect our balance sheet. But when we consider the continued loss of wetlands in America, few projects have been more rewarding than this one." Here, the admission of the capitalist drive behind Chevron becomes a claim for a more "authentic" concern for the environment, a claim that allows the corporation to seem especially altruistic. The unstated—but clearly implicit—message is that buying Chevron gasoline is participating in the protection of the environment and the further maintenance of America's endangered wetlands.

Phillips 66, a petroleum company, makes similar claims to environmental protection in its advertisements. One features a wooded area in autumn, red leaves covering the ground, yellow and orange leaves hanging on trees in the background. The headline reads: "Because we'll recycle over 200 million plastic bottles this year, landfills can be filled with other things. Like land, for instance." The copy explains that Phillips also runs a plastics recycling plant that will help "do more to protect what we have" by "reduc[ing] landfill waste and conserv[ing] natural resources." Once again, public concern about environmental protection is transferred from the formal political realm to the everyday realm of consumption.

Advertisements have long claimed remarkable, even impossible, feats for their products, and the idea that they now conflate consumption with political action may not seem particularly dangerous. In the transition from class society to risk society, which continually generates the cultural need for the ideology of the alternative that sustains the public sphere of alternative health, issues of class and equality are obscured by the commodification of bodily practices and the discourses that position them as antidotes to the emergent risks of modernity. The individualization of modern society motivates the

New Age fascination with self-discovery and self-healing, a disturbing trend toward self-absorption that enables people to transfer concern about other members of society to concern for the environment at large. Despite the fact that the commodified discourses which constitute the public sphere of alternative health sound and feel and seem political, consumption is not political action. Believing it to be so is perhaps the greatest risk of modernity.

Notes

Chapter 1. Ideology Incorporated

1. Biographical information about Mani and Alan Finger is taken from Stephanie Golden, "Like Father, Like Son: Looking for a Way to Live a Sane Life in a 'Crazy City,' New Yorkers Are Flocking to Mani and Alan Finger's Ishta Yoga," *Yoga Journal*, Aug. 1994, 36-38 and 40.

2. Duns and Bradstreet-Duns Market Identifiers (Dialog File 516).

3. Robert Cantwell, *Ethnomimesis: Folklore and the Representation of Culture* (Chapel Hill: University of North Carolina Press, 1993). Cantwell pushes the idea of mimesis beyond the realms of language, orality, literature, and aesthetics where it most commonly occurs and into the domains of folkloristic practice and public display. In adding the prefix "ethno-" to the concept of mimesis, he makes explicit the often unarticulated but central relationship of mimesis to issues of alterity and power. See also Michael Taussig, *Mimesis and Alterity* (London: Routledge, 1993), and Gunter Gebauer and Christoph Wulf, *Mimesis: Culture, Art, Society*, trans. Don Reneau (Berkeley: University of California Press, 1995 [1992]), 1-24 and 315-320, for more on mimesis and power.

4. Taussig, xiii.

5. Gebauer and Wulf, 5.

6. See, for instance, Ann Douglas, *The Feminization of American Culture* (New York: Knopf, 1977); T. J. Jackson Lears, *No Place of Grace: Antimodernism and the Transformation of American Culture, 1880-1920* (New York: Pantheon Books, 1981); Dominick Cavallo, *Muscles and Morals: Organized Playgrounds and Urban Reform, 1880-1920* (Philadelphia: University of Pennsylvania Press, 1981).

7. For more on Muscular Christianity, see Harvey Green, *Fit for America: Health, Fitness, Sport, and American Society* (New York: Pantheon Books, 1986), and Cavallo.

8. Green, 182.

9. Green, 181-182.

10. Green, 182.

11. See Benedict Anderson, *Imagined Communities: Reflections on the Origin and Spread of Nationalism* (London: Verso, 1983) for how such imagined social and collective realities are constructed through popular discourses.

12. Gebauer and Wulf, 2.

13. See Green for more on the history of physical education programs, Roberta J. Park, "Healthy, Moral, and Strong: Educational Views of Exercise and Athletics in Nineteenth-Century America," in *Fitness in American Culture: Images of Health, Sport, and the Body, 1830-1940*, ed. Kathryn Grover (Amherst: University of Massachusetts Press, 1989) for more on the history of physical education, the YMCA, and other public gymnasiums, and Cavallo for more on the history of city playgrounds.

14. See, for instance, Michelle Stacey, *Consumed: Why Americans Love, Hate, and Fear Food* (New York: Touchstone Books, 1994); James C. Whorton, "Eating to Win: Popular Concepts of Diet, Strength, and Energy in the Early Twentieth Century," in *Fitness in American Culture*, ed. Kathryn Grover (Amherst: University of Massachusetts Press, 1989), 86-122, and Warren J. Belasco, *Appetite for Change* (New York: Pantheon Books, 1989).

15. Green, 284.

16. See, for example, the Yoga Zone catalog, which offers t-shirts, sweatshirts, and baseball caps with the company's logo, and the Living Arts catalog, which offers Om jewelry.

17. Robert B. Tisserand, *The Art of Aromatherapy* (Rochester: Healing Arts Press, 1985 [1977]), 6.

18. Aveline Kushi and Wendy Esko, *The Quick and Natural Macrobiotic Cookbook* (Chicago: Contemporary Books, 1989), 25.

19. Edward Said, *Orientalism* (New York: Pantheon Books, 1978).

20. J. J. Clarke, *Oriental Enlightenment: The Encounter Between Asian and Western Thought* (London: Routledge, 1997), 7-9.

21. Clarke, 9.

22. Clarke, 19.

23. Clarke, 31-33 and 173-178.

24. Ted J. Kaptchuk makes a similar argument with respect to the introduction of alternative health movements: "The rise of the mar-

ket economy and industrialization allowed for nostalgia and a romantic view of nature, which made possible the natural healing movements that date from the early nineteenth century. Alternative healing movement 'irregulars' launched crusades to overthrow the orthodox medicine 'regulars,' who used contaminated and poisonous 'drugs and bleeding.' (Warner cited in Ted J. Kaptchuk, "Historical Context of the Concept of Vitalism in Complementary and Alternative Medicine," in *Fundamentals of Complementary and Alternative Medicine*, ed. Marc S. Micozzi [New York: Churchill Livingstone, 1996], 41.) The example of alternative health movements coheres with Clarke's notion of Eastern philosophies as subversive countermovements when invoked in Western contexts. For popular alternative health options like aromatherapy, macrobiotic eating, yoga, and t'ai chi, however, the potential for subversive and substantial alternative paradigms of health and wellness is undermined by the processes by which these practices are made into commodities for a market economy.

25. Ulrich Beck, *Risk Society*, trans. Mark Ritter (London: Sage Publications, 1992).

26. For Beck, risk society is fundamentally related to reflexive modernization: "The concept of risk is directly bound to the concept of reflexive modernization. *Risk* may be defined as a *systematic way of dealing with hazards and insecurities induced and introduced by modernization itself.* Risks, as opposed to older dangers, are consequences which relate to the threatening force of modernization and to its globalization of doubt. They are *politically reflexive*" (21; emphasis in original).

27. Beck, 74.

28. Craig Calhoun, *Habermas and the Public Sphere* (Cambridge: MIT Press, 1996 [1992]), 21.

29. Habermas' conception of the public sphere is strictly sociopolitical in its focus on the politics and philosophy of democracy. However, a number of theorists have pushed the concept beyond Habermas's interest in the ideal mechanics of a democratic polity (e.g., Alexander 1995, Austin 1995, Boyd 1995, Warner 1996 [1992], Zaret 1996 [1992]) and beyond his elite and singular model, conceiving of multiple, overlapping, at times competing, public spheres (e.g., Baker, Jr. 1995, Dawson 1995, Fraser 1996 [1992], Gilroy 1995, Gregory 1995, Ryan 1996 [1992]).

30. Stuart Hall, "The Local and the Global: Globalization and Ethnicity" and "Old and New Identities, Old and New Ethnicities," both in *Culture, Globalization and the World-System: Contemporary Conditions for the Representation of Identity*, ed. Anthony D. King (Binghamton: State University of New York Press, 1991), 19-39 and 41-68. Quotations from 28, 31, 33.

31. Stuart Hall, "Notes on Deconstructing 'The Popular,'" in *People's History and Socialist History*, ed. Samuel Raphael (London: Routledge and Kegan Paul, 1981), 228-233.

32. See also Dell Hymes, "Folklore's Nature and the Sun's Myth," *Journal of American Folklore* 88 (1975): 345-369 for his perspective on traditionalization. Hymes describes traditionalization as a process and a universal need: "It seems in fact the case that every person, and group, makes some effort to 'traditionalize' aspects of its experience. To 'traditionalize' would seem to be a universal need. Groups and persons differ, then, not in presence or absence of the traditional—there are none which do not 'traditionalize'—but in the degree, and the form, of success in satisfying the universal need" (354). As an ethnolinguist, Hymes emphasizes the process of traditionalization as an emic one, specifically the personal or group perception and presentation of different vernacular experiences. Both Hymes and Hall challenge the idea that tradition is static—a body of expressive culture—and posit more dynamic, processual ways of understanding tradition and of studying expressive culture. I am building in particular on Hymes's use of "traditionalization" both as an emic process of definition and as an etic category of analysis by considering the ways in which it is used in mediated cultural productions.

33. Hall, "Deconstructing the Popular," 236-237.

34. See, for instance, Grant McCracken, *Culture and Consumption: New Approaches to the Symbolic Character of Consumer Goods and Activities* (Bloomington: Indiana University Press, 1988); Mike Featherstone, *Consumer Culture and Postmodernism* (London: Sage Publications, 1991); Colin Campbell, "The Sociology of Consumption," in *Acknowledging Consumption*, ed. Daniel Miller (London: Routledge, 1991); Peter K. Lunt and Sonia M. Livingstone, *Mass Consumption and Personal Identity: Everyday Economic Experience* (Philadelphia: Open University Press, 1992); Rob Shields, ed., *Lifestyle Shopping: The Subject of Consumption* (New York: Routledge, 1992).

35. Shields, 16.

36. Pierre Bourdieu, *Distinction: A Social Critique of the Judgement of Taste*, trans. Richard Nice (Cambridge: Harvard University Press, 1984), 101-109.

37. Bourdieu seeks to articulate the logic of consumption as expressed through cultural practices and preferences. He emphasizes the fact that taste (or manifested cultural preferences) is not a natural faculty. Rather, he argues that it has been naturalized by social groups at the top of the hierarchy as an ideological mode of maintaining social position.

38. Malcolm Gladwell, "Annals of Style: The Coolhunt," *New Yorker*, 17 March 1997: 77-88, quote on 81. Gladwell provides some of the background to this phenomenon: "Some say it was all about the early and visible endorsement given Hilfiger by the hip-hop auteur Grand Puba, who wore a dark-green-and-blue Tommy jacket over a white Tommy T-shirt as he leaned on his black Lamborghini on the cover of the hugely influential 'Grand Puba 2000' CD, and whose love for Hilfiger soon spread to other rappers. (Who could forget the rhymes of Mobb Deep? 'Tommy was my nigga/And couldn't figure/How me and Hilfiger/used to move through with vigor.')"

39. McCracken, 134.

40. Jean Baudrillard, *The System of Objects*, trans. James Benedict (New York: Verso, 1996 [1968]), 175.

41. McCracken, 104-117.

42. McCracken, 110. See also Susan Willis, *Primer for Daily Life* (New York: Routledge, 1991), for a discussion of consumer culture, product packaging, and anticipation and desire, and Susan Stewart, *On Longing: Narratives of the Miniature, the Gigantic, the Souvenir, the Collection* (Baltimore: Johns Hopkins University Press, 1984) for a discussion of longing and collecting.

43. Desire for objects is at the heart of consumption and may have its origins in a variety of sources, none mutually exclusive—displaced meaning, belief in the object's expressed ideology, drives to refashion one's identity, a need to mark one's social distinction. See Georg Simmel, *The Philosophy of Money*, trans. Tom Bottomore and David Frisby (Boston: Routledge and Kegan Paul, 1978 [1906]). For Simmel, it is through the creation and maintenance of desire that the value of an object is determined, and he briefly notes that such desire derives

from the separation of subject and object, a separation which exists only because the opposite condition is "represented in stylized form by the concept of Paradise" (75). Here, Simmel foreshadows McCracken's notion of desire as evoked by displaced meaning.

44. My point here is to highlight the complexity of the relationship to ensure that I have not given the impression of the public shere of alternative health as a totalizing system.

45. Robert Goldman, *Reading Ads Socially* (London: Routledge, 1992), 1.

46. See, for instance, Green, Stacey, and Kaptchuk.

Chapter 2. Aromatherapy

1. Robert Tisserand, *The Art of Aromatherapy* (Rochester, Vt.: Healing Arts Press, 1985 [1977]), 8.

2. Susanne Fischer-Rizzi, *Complete Aromatherapy Handbook: Essential Oils for Radiant Health* (New York: Sterling, 1990), 12.

3. For more details and descriptions of general aromatic practices in ancient Egyptian, Greek, Roman, and Persian cultures, see Charles F. Myer, "The Use of Aromatics in Ancient Mesopotamia," Ph.D. diss., University of Pennsylvania, 1975. Ann Arbor: University Microfilms International, 1975. AAC 7612314 and Constance Classen, David Howes, and Anthony Synnott, *Aroma: The Cultural History of Smell* (London: Routledge, 1994).

4. Tisserand, 22 and Classen, Howes, and Synnott, 15.

5. As quoted in Tisserand, 22 and Classen, Howes, and Synnott, 15.

6. Classen, Howes, and Synnott, 26.

7. Classen, Howes, and Synnott, 26.

8. Tisserand, 20.

9. The two recipes and Tisserand's comments are as follows (Tisserand, 20-21):

> Here is a recipe for eye inflammation (translated from hieroglyphics):
> Myrrh, "Great Protectors" seed, Copper Oxide, Lemon pips, Northern cypress flowers, Antimony, Gazelle's droppings, Oryx offal, White Oil.
> The directions for use are as follows:
> Place in water, let stand for one night, strain through a cloth, and smear over eye for four days.

Myrrh is still used today as an anti-inflammatory agent. Here is a recipe for a cosmetic face pack, from the same papyrus:

Ball of incense, wax, fresh oil, cypress berries; Crush, and rub down and put in new milk and apply it to the face for six days.

The incense would refer to myrrh, or frankincense, or a mixture of the two. It was made into small balls for burning in a type of censer. This recipe bears an amazing resemblance to modern nature face packs.

10. Myer, 13.

11. Hasnain Walji, *The Healing Power of Aromatherapy: The Enlightened Person's Guide to the Physical, Emotional, and Spiritual Benefits of Essential Oils* (Rocklin, Calif.: Prima Publications, 1996), 10.

12. Myer, 14.

13. Tisserand, 23.

14. Classen, Howes, and Synnott, 15.

15. Quoted in Classen, Howes, and Synnott, 17 and Tisserand, 26.

16. Classen, Howes, and Synnott, 45.

17. Classen, Howes, and Synnott, 47.

18. Classen, Howes, and Synnott, 48.

19. Tisserand, 26-27.

20. Classen, Howes, and Synnott, 41.

21. Tisserand, 27.

22. Pliny describes a range of diverse remedies in his *Natural History* (cited in Classen, Howes, and Synnott, 41): "Rue in vinegar was given to comatose patients to smell as a kind of smelling salt. Epileptics were treated with the scent of thyme. The smell of pennyroyal was held to protect the head from cold or heat and to lessen thirst. The scent of a sprig of pennyroyal wrapped in wool was believed to help sufferers from recurrent fevers, while the odour of pennyroyal seeds was employed for cases of speech loss. Mint scent was thought to refresh the spirit. It was also commonly used to ease stomachaches.... The smell of the *carum capticum* plant was said to help women conceive, while the smell of anise ensured an easier childbirth. Anise was also thought to relieve sleepiness and hiccoughs through its odour and, when boiled with celery, sneezing. Fumigation with bay leaves, in turn, was considered to ward off the contaminating odours of disease."

23. For more on the ancient Palestinian use of aromatics, see Myer.

24. Real Goods, Summer 1997 catalogue, 17. The catalogue does not cite its source, and I have not come across any other references to Native American aromatherapy.

25. Tisserand, 5-6.

26. Tisserand, 7, 6

27. Classen, Howes, and Synnott, 38.

28. Tisserand, 6-7.

29. Walji, 9.

30. Tisserand, 8, 45.

31. Walji, 2.

32. Walji, 16.

33. Fischer-Rizzi, 9.

34. Rebecca Piirto Heath, "Beyond the Fringe in the 1990s," *American Demographics*, June 1997, 27.

35. All prices quoted in this chapter are from 1997.

36. Shelley M. Colwell, "Aromatherapy: Waiting to Inhale," *Soap-Cosmetics-Chemical Specialties*, Dec. 1996, 35.

37. Market Intelligence Service, Ltd., "Bath & Body Works Aromatherapy Linen Spray—Pure Refreshment," *Market Intelligence Survey, Ltd. Product Alert* 13 (1997): 1.

38. Liz Parks, "Scents for the Soul: Aromatherapy Line Aims at Mass Market," *Drug Store News*, 16 June 1997, 1.

39. Even the naming highlights the orientalist logic at work here. Green tea is primarily a Japanese product and the equation of Green Tea with enlightenment implies an association with zen philosophy and practice. Of course, the absence of any substantial zen, or even Japanese, connection underscores the ways in which the "orient" is invoked as a romanticized means of escaping from Western modernity.

40. Parks, 1.

41. Of course, the creation of new products and new "needs" is not unique to Bath & Body Works. One woman recently pointed out the irony of Origins' (the department store line of natural products) recycling program. All Origins product labels state that the container should be returned to Origins so that it can be refilled with the same product. However, this woman says that she often returns the container only to find that that specific product has been discontinued

and replaced by something similar (and, undoubtedly, newer and better), which comes in a different container.

42. Lori Bongiorno, "Beth Pritchard Has Big Plans for Bath & Body Works," *Business Week*, 4 Aug. 1997, 79.

43. Tisserand, 297–306.

44. Fischer-Rizzi, 9.

45. Ulrich Beck, *Risk Society*, translated by Mark Ritter (London: Sage Publications, 1992), 49, 30.

46. Fischer-Rizzi, 9.

47. Tisserand, 76.

48. Colwell, 35.

49. Anastasia Alexander, founder of Aroma Therapeutics, quoted in Colwell, 35.

50. Christine Malcolm, "In Search of Rare Essences for Green-Minded Consumers. Fragrances and Flavors," *Drug and Cosmetic Industry*, May 1994, 24.

51. Fionnuala McHugh, "Taking Lauder Back to Nature," *South China Morning Post*, 22 Jan. 1997, Style sec., p. 19. In November 1997, the Estée Lauder Companies Inc. purchased Aveda for $300 million. Rechelbacher remains the chairman of Aveda and sees the sale to the Estée Lauder Companies Inc. as a continuation of Aveda's commitment to "[bring] the Aveda philosophy to as many consumers as possible." For more details on Estée Lauder's purchase of Aveda, see PR Newswire, "The Estée Lauder Companies Inc. to Acquire Aveda Corporation, Leading Hair and Beauty Company," *PR Newswire Association, Inc.*, 19 Nov. 1997, and Dana Canedy, "Estée Lauder Is Acquiring Maker of Natural Cosmetics," *New York Times*, 20 Nov. 1997, sec. D, p. 4.

52. *Incentive* 1997: 73.

53. Beck, 21, emphasis in original.

54. Parks, 175.

55. Quoted in Parks, 175.

56. Beck, 56.

57. Colwell, 35.

58. Kimberly J. Lau, "The Social Failure of the Feminist Movement: A Rhetorical Analysis of Women's Magazines," B.A. honors thesis, University of California, Berkeley, 1990.

59. Colwell, 35.

60. Quoted in Doug Grow, "Smelling Good Can Be Trouble," *Minneapolis-St. Paul Tribune*, 9 Nov. 1994, sec. F, p. 8.

61. L. M. Sixel, "Businesses Try to Limit Fragrances. Move Delights Sensitive Workers," *Houston Chronicle*, 2 Feb. 1995, sec. B, p. 1.

62. Sixel, B1.

63. For more details, see Ingrid Becker, "Coalition Claims Protection from Fragrances under ADA," *Marin Independent Journal*, 27 Jan. 1992, p. 1, and Amy Knutson-Strack, "CTFA [Cosmetic, Toiletry, and Fragrance Association] Scientific Conference and Annual Trade Show: Adverse Reactions and Claims," *Cosmetics and Toiletries*, Feb. 1997, 35.

64. Sixel, B1.

65. See, for instance, Suzanne Rostler, "Anti-Scent Sentiment Catching on in Offices," *Cleveland Plain Dealer*, 16 July 1993, sec. E, p. 1 as well as Becker, Grow, and Sixel.

66. Grow, 8F.

67. Rostler, 1E.

68. Quoted in Rostler, 1E.

69. Quoted in the Aveda webpage: *http://www.aveda.com*, 1997.

70. For more on the ways in which temporal and spatial distancing reproduce colonialist paradigms in anthropological thought, see Johannes Fabian, *Time and the Other: How Anthropology Makes Its Object* (New York: Columbia University Press, 1983).

71. Michio Kushi and Edward Esko, *Holistic Health Through Macrobiotics* (New York: Japan Publications, Inc., 1993), 69.

72. The very presence of James Frazer's classic *The Golden Bough* (1911) in many bookstores, occult shops, and botanicas attests to the extensive interest in finding ancient rituals for modern society. Perhaps the greatest spokesperson for this new ritual movement is Robert Bly, poet and leader of the men's movement. In formulating ways for men to overcome the psychological damage incurred by cultural trends like remote fathers, radical feminism, and negative media portrayals of men, Bly popularizes Victor Turner's anthropological work with ritual to create new initiation rites in which men can "start seeing the Wild Man" (Robert Bly, *Iron John: A Book About Men* [New York: Vintage, 1990], 180-207; Victor Turner, *A Forest of Symbols* [Ithaca: Cornell University Press, 1970]; Victor Turner, *The Ritual Process* [Ithaca: Cornell University Press, 1977]). Together with Irish

storyteller Michael Meade and "renegade psychologist" James Hillman, "one of the world's foremost Jungian thinkers," Bly offers workshops in which men beat drums, scream, and chant as part of the ritual process which helps them reach a place of security and self-realization (Don Lattin, "Just Men Being (New) Men: Poet Robert Bly's Gatherings Are Modern Versions of Initiation Rites," *San Francisco Chronicle*, 15 March 1990, sec. B, p. 3). Even more recently, Bly has begun to move beyond the men's movement in calling for more rites of passage, initiations on a broad cultural level, which would remedy the lack of "verticality"—the nature of the line which connects "the realms of wisdom and truth with the realms of ancestors and elders" —in our society, a lack which has led to a nation of "siblings" and "adolescents" (Joy Farr, "Of Swords, Words and the Necessity of Elders: It's Time for a New Generation of Mentors to Awaken the Spirit of Inspiration in the Young," *Press Enterprise*, 9 Oct. 1997, sec. E, p. 1). Ultimately, it is through this type of revived and reinvented ritual process that New Age discourses access the iconic spirituality of "ancient times" to market products and workshops designed to address the absence of ritual which they have simultaneously identified as one of the primary sources of social disease.

Chapter 3. Macrobiotic Eating

1. George Ohsawa, *Essential Ohsawa: From Food to Health, Happiness to Freedom*, ed. Carl Ferré (Garden City Park, N.Y.: Avery, 1994), 1.

2. Stephen Blauer, introduction to *The Macrobiotic Way: The Complete Macrobiotic Diet and Exercise Book*, by Michio Kushi and Stephen Blauer (Garden Park City, N.Y.: Avery, 1985), xi.

3. Michio Kushi and Edward Esko, *Holistic Health Through Macrobiotics* (New York: Japan Publications, 1993), 362.

4. *http://www.turq.com/macroto/people.html*, 1997.

5. Blauer, xii.

6. Duns and Bradstreet–Duns Market Identifiers (Dialog File 516).

7. Kushi's own promotional materials (i.e., catalog and webpage) characterize the Kushi Institute and the East West Foundation as nonprofit organizations devoted to macrobiotic education, but business reports in Duns Market Identifiers (Dialog File 516) suggest that

both may be for-profit businesses. Both are characterized as corporations, and the East West Foundation is reported to have done $950,000 in sales during 1997.

8. Mary Ellen Kuhn, "Courting Crossover Vegetarian Consumers," *Food Processing*, June 1996, 26-31.

9. The public television show is called *Cooking with Christina.* Christina Pirello, the chef and star of the show as well as a cancer survivor who attributes her healing to macrobiotic living, is also the author of a cookbook titled *Cooking the Whole Foods Way: Your Complete, Everyday Guide to Healthy, Delicious Eating with Five Hundred Recipes* (New York: Berkley Publishing Group, 1997).

10. *http://www.macronews.com/tours2.htm*, 1997.

11. M. Kushi and E. Esko, 247-299, quotations on 5, 258.

12. M. Kushi and E. Esko, 249. Unless noted otherwise, references to Kushi and Esko in the text will refer to Michio Kushi and Edward Esko. When I am referring to the collaborative works of Aveline Kushi and Wendy Esko, I will use their first initials as well as their surnames.

13. M. Kushi and E. Esko, 249-250.

14. M. Kushi and E. Esko, 261.

15. M. Kushi and E. Esko, 263.

16. M. Kushi and E. Esko, 21.

17. Barbara Rossi and Glory Schloss, *Everyday Macrobiotic Cookbook* (New York: Universal, 1971), 14-15; and M. Kushi and E. Esko, 20.

18. *http://www.macrobiotics.org/DietOrderYY.html*, 1997.

19. *http://www.macrobiotics.org/DietOrderYY.html*, 1997.

20. *http://www.macrobiotics.org/DietOrderYY.html*, 1997.

21. Aveline Kushi and Wendy Esko, *The Quick and Natural Macrobiotic Cookbook* (Chicago: Contemporary Books, 1989), 35-47 and 65-100; Rossi and Schloss, 15-16; Kushi and Blauer, 86-90; M. Kushi and E. Esko, 136-140.

22. *http://www.macrobiotics.org/DietOrderYY.html*, 1997.

23. M. Kushi and E. Esko, 281.

24. Kushi and Blauer, 106-109 and M. Kushi and E. Esko, 282-283. Some of the logic is a bit circular here; after all, "living each day happily" and "keeping all relationships smooth and happy" don't seem much different than "living happier, more fulfilling lives."

25. M. Kushi and E. Esko, 284.

26. M. Kushi and E. Esko, 284-286, 292, 299.

27. Rossi and Schloss, 11-13; Kushi and Blauer, 1-2, 10-12, and 23-24; A. Kushi and W. Esko, 3-4 and 12-15; M. Kushi and E. Esko, 50-54.

28. Ohsawa quoted in Carl Ferré, "Introducing Essential Ohsawa" excerpted by Ferré for *Macrobiotics Today*, Sept.-Oct. 1994, online version; my emphasis. *http://www.natural-connection.com/resource/default.html.*

29. M. Kushi and E. Esko, 319; my emphasis.

30. Kushi and Blauer, xvii; my emphasis.

31. A. Kushi and W. Esko, 25; my emphasis.

32. Kushi and Blauer, 59.

33. A. Kushi and W. Esko, 25.

34. Colin Spencer, *The Heretic's Feast: A History of Vegetarianism* (London: Fourth Estate, 1993), 32, 90.

35. Spencer, 180, 182-183. Of course, these menus are slightly exaggerated due to the fact that the only remaining menus are from feasts hosted by the wealthier members of society.

36. A. Kushi and W. Esko, 26-27; and Kushi and Blauer, xvii and 1-2.

37. A. Kushi and W. Esko, 26.

38. Kushi and Blauer, xvii.

39. Alexander Leaf, "A Scientist Visits Some of the World's Oldest People: 'Every Day Is a Gift When You Are Over 100'," *National Geographic*, Jan. 1973, 92-102.

40. Rossi and Schloss, 9, 18.

41. M. Kushi and E. Esko, 299, 352.

42. Michelle Stacey, *Consumed: Why Americans Love, Hate, and Fear Food* (New York: Touchstone Books, 1994), 12-13.

43. Quoted in Stacey, 13.

44. Quoted in Stacey, 49.

45. Stacey, 23.

46. Schwartz quoted in Stacey, 23.

47. Stacey, 116.

48. Spencer, 32, 55-57, quotations on 32, 118.

49. M. Kushi and E. Esko, 292-293, 298.

50. M. Kushi and E. Esko, 298.

51. Rossi and Schloss, 17-18.

52. Kushi and Blauer, 199.

53. Stacey, 15 and 85-129.

54. Stacey, 90.

55. Quoted in Stacey, 178.

56. Stacey, 179.

57. Polivy and Herman quoted in Stacey, 179.

58. Susan Bordo, *Unbearable Weight: Feminism, Western Culture, and the Body* (Berkeley: University of California Press, 1993).

59. Stacey, 173, 182-187, quotation on 184.

60. Kushi and Blauer, 24.

61. Kushi and Blauer, 24-25.

91 Z'ev Rosenberg, "It's Your Metabolism, Not Your Diet." *Macrobiotics Today*, July-Aug. 1994, online version. *http://www.natural-connection.com/resource/default.html.*

63. Quoted in Stacey, 184.

64. M. Kushi and E. Esko, 289.

65. Stacey, 23.

66. M. Kushi and E. Esko, 289.

67. Rossi and Schloss, 11-12.

68. Benedict quoted in Kushi and Blauer, 38.

69. M. Kushi and E. Esko, 290-291.

70. Kushi and Blauer, 9-10.

71. George Ohsawa, 1.

72. Rossi and Schloss, 13.

73. Johannes Fabian, *Time and the Other: How Anthropology Makes Its Object* (New York: Columbia University Press, 1983), 30-32.

74. See also Renato Rosaldo, "Imperialist Nostalgia," *Representations* 26 (Spring 1989): 107-122. Rosaldo posits the idea of "imperialist nostalgia" as a longing for and veneration of what one has participated in destroying.

75. National Academy of Sciences, in M. Kushi and Blauer, 26.

76. *http://www.macrobiotics.org/CancerScientific.html*; Kushi and Blauer, 33-36; A. Kushi and W. Esko, 16-22; M. Kushi and E. Esko, 304-332.

77. Kushi and Blauer, 27.

78. Kushi and Blauer, 26-27.

79. Stacey, 174.

80. Kushi and Blauer, 116.

81. See Homi Bhabha, *The Location of Culture* (London: Routledge, 1994), 77, for more on the process by which the continual remaking of stereotypes grants them social power.

82. Daniel Stern, "Macrobiotic Meals Get 'Ritzy,'" *Washington Post*, 27 Aug. 1997, Food Sec., p. 1.

Chapter 4. Yoga and T'ai Chi

1. Arieh Lev Breslow, *Beyond the Closed Door: Chinese Culture and the Creation of T'ai Chi Ch'uan* (Jerusalem: Almond Blossom Press, 1995); Sophia Delza, *The T'ai Chi Ch'uan Experience: Reflections and Perceptions on Body-Mind Harmony* (Albany: State University of New York Press, 1996); John Ball, *Ananda: Where Yoga Lives* (Bowling Green: Bowling Green University Press, 1982); Wendell Thomas, *Hinduism Invades America* (New York: Beacon Press, 1930); Yogananda, *Autobiography of a Yogi* (Los Angeles: Self-Realization Fellowship, 1993 [1946]); Alan Lopez, *Reality Construction in an Eastern Mystical Cult* (New York: Garland, 1992).

2. Georg Feuerstein, *Textbook of Yoga* (London: Rider, 1975), 3.

3. Feuerstein, 42.

4. Feuerstein, 32.

5. Lopez, 7.

6. Feuerstein, 45-46.

7. Feuerstein, 57-58.

8. Feuerstein, 70-71, and Moti Lal Pandit, *Towards Transcendence: A Historico-Analytical Study of Yoga as a Method of Liberation* (New Delhi: Intercultural, 1991), xiv-xv.

9. Feuerstein, 71-72, 70.

10. Feuerstein, 71, 72, 73.

11. Feuerstein, 73-81 and Pandit, 14-20.

12. Pandit, vx.

13. Feuerstein, 83, and Georg Feuerstein, *The Yoga-Sūtra of Patañjali* (Folkstone, Kent, England: Wm. Dawson, 1979), viii.

14. Feuerstein, *Yoga Sūtra*, 6, 17.

15. Feuerstein *Yoga Sūtra*, 17 and Pandit, xvi-xvii.

16. Pandit, xv-xxii.

17. Anne Cushman, "Iyengar Looks Back," *Yoga Journal*, Nov.-Dec. 1997, 86, 90, 91.

18. Iyengar quoted in Cushman, 159.

19. Cushman, 87.

20. Thomas, 72-78; and Kirin Narayan, "Refractions of the Field at

Home: American Representations of Hindu Holy Men in the Nineteenth and Twentieth Centuries," *Cultural Anthropology* 8 (1993): 492.

21. Thomas, 79, 85-86, quotation on 81.

22. Quoted in Thomas, 101.

23. Ball, 17 and Yogananda, 399-417.

24. Ball, 183 and Yogananda, 275-285.

25. For detailed ethnographies of such communal living, see Ball and Lopez.

26. Iyengar quoted in Cushman, 160.

27. Paul H. Crompton, *The Art of T'ai Chi* (Rockport, Mass.: Element, 1993), ix and Alfred Huang, *T'ai Chi: The Definitive Guide to Physical and Emotional Self-Improvement* (Boston: Charles E. Tuttle, 1993), 46, quotation on xi.

28. Breslow, 205, 206.

29. Breslow, 202-203.

30. Breslow, 207.

31. Breslow, 208-209; Crompton, x-xi; Waysun Liao, *T'ai Chi Classics* (Boston: Shambhala, 1990), viii.

32. Breslow, 209, and Crompton, xi.

33. Breslow, 210.

34. Breslow, 211, 218.

35. Breslow, quotations on 211, 212, 213.

36. Crompton, xii, xiii.

37. Breslow, 218-219, quotation on 219.

38. Crompton, 3.

39. Breslow, 225-227.

40. Crompton, 4, quotation on 4.

41. Crompton, 5, 6-7.

42. Breslow, 242 and 258-261 and Crompton, 7-11.

43. Breslow, 32-35 and Crompton, 8.

44. Crompton, 8.

45. Crompton, 9, quotation on 10.

46. See, for instance, Bruce F. Campbell, *Ancient Wisdom Revived: A History of the Theosophical Movement* (Berkeley: University of California Press, 1980); Carl Jackson, *The Oriental Religions and American Thought* (Westport, Conn.: Greenwood Press, 1981); Jean Sedlar, *India in the Mind of Germany: Schelling, Schopenhauer and Their*

Times (Washington, D.C.: University Press of America, 1982); A. Leslie Willson, *A Mythical Image: The Ideal of India in German Romanticism* (Durham, N.C.: Duke University Press, 1964).

47. Regina Bendix, *In Search of Authenticity: The Foundation of Folklore Studies* (Madison: University of Wisconsin Press, 1997), 55-58.

48. On orientalist fixation with the exotic, see Arjun Appadurai, "Putting Hierarchy in Its Place," *Cultural Anthropology* 3 (1988): 36-49; J. J. Clarke, *Oriental Enlightenment: The Encounter Between Asian and Western Thought* (London: Routledge, 1997); Edward Said, *Orientalism* (New York: Pantheon Books, 1978); Renato Rosaldo, "Imperialist Nostalgia," *Representations* 26 (Spring 1989): 107-122. On Transcendentalism see Bendix, 68-76; Julie Ellison, *Emerson's Romantic Style* (Princeton: Princeton University Press, 1984); Ralph Waldo Emerson, *The Collected Works of Ralph Waldo Emerson*, vol. 1 (Cambridge, Mass.: Belknap Press of Harvard University, 1971); Alan D. Hodder, *Emerson's Rhetoric of Revelation: Nature, the Reader, and the Apocalypse Within* (University Park: Pennsylvania State University Press, 1989); Jackson; Narayan, 489-490.

49. Narayan, 488-491.

50. Cushman, 86.

51. Roger Abrahams, "Phantoms of Romantic Nationalism in Folkloristics," *Journal of American Folklore* 106 (1993): 3-37; Bendix, 48-49; Alan Dundes, "Nationalistic Inferiority Complexes and the Fabrication of Folklore," *Journal of Folklore Research* 22 (1985): 5-18; Richard Handler, *Nationalism and the Politics of Culture in Quebec* (Madison: University of Wisconsin Press, 1988); Michael Herzfeld, *Ours Once More: Folklore, Ideology, and the Making of Modern Greece* (Austin: University of Texas Press, 1982); William A. Wilson, *Folklore, Nationalism and Politics in Modern Finland* (Bloomington: Indiana University Press, 1976).

52. Michele Bitoun Blecher, "Executive Health and Fitness: From Left-of-Center to the Executive Suite: Meditation, Yoga and Other Mind-Body Exercises Find Business Audience," *Crain's Chicago Business*, 20 Jan. 1997, sec. H, p. 1; Marie-Claude Lortie, "Lotus Blossoms: Demystified Yoga Becomes a Growth Industry," *Los Angeles Times*, 19 June 1997, sec. D, p. 1; John Brant, "Power Yoga—A New Form of an Ancient Practice Builds Strength and Endurance," *Seattle Times*, 31

Jan. 1996, sec. E, p. 1; Susan G. Reinhardt, "Yoga Class Is a Fun Class at Gold's," *Asheville Citizen Times*, 28 Nov. 1995, sec. C, p. 5; Beryl Bender Birch, *Power Yoga: The Total Strength and Flexibility Workout* (New York: Simon and Schuster, 1995), 22-23.

53. Vezina quoted in Charles Laurence, "Wellbeing: You Don't Need Weights and Machines to Work Out. Charles Laurence Watches New Yorkers Being Put Through Their Paces in Central Park," *Daily Telegraph*, 10 Oct. 1997, 22.

54. Kochek quoted in Reinhardt, C5.

55. Alice Christensen, *The American Yoga Association's New Yoga Challenge: Powerful Workouts for Flexibility, Strength, Energy, and Inner Discovery* (Lincolnwood, Ill.: Contemporary Books, 1997), 75.

56. Breslow, 301.

57. Crompton, vii-viii.

58. Robert B. Tisserand, *The Art of Aromatherapy* (Rochester, Vt.: Healing Arts Press, 1985 [1977]), 5-6.

59. Claire Hooton, *T'ai Chi for Beginners: Ten Minutes to Health and Fitness* (New York: Berkley, 1996), 6.

60. Newhouse News Service, "Destroyer or Savior? Impending Yantze Dam Divides Chinese People," *St. Louis Post-Dispatch*, 28 Dec. 1997, sec. A, p. 5, and Rose Tang, "No Turning Back Now: For Good or Ill, China's Three Gorges Dam Moves Ahead," *Asiaweek*, Nov. 1997, 42.

61. Nancy Ross-Flanigan, "It's Only Natural: Psychologists Studying Humans' Relationship with Environment," *Dallas Morning News*, 18 Dec. 1996, sec. D, p. 8. The ecopsychologist Robert Greenway quoted on 8D.

62. Lortie, D1.

63. Breslow, 337-338.

64. *http://www.ecoville.com/maple-ki*, 1997.

65. *http://www.ecoville.com/maple-ki*, 1997.

66. *http://www.nosara.com/retreat*, 1997.

67. Sharon Herbstman; "Paradise Ain't Perfect: Sivananda Ashram Yoga Retreat," *Women's Sports and Fitness*, March 1997, 32.

68. Breslow, 305.

69. *http://www.nosara.com/retreat*, 1997.

70. *Healing Retreats and Spas* 1998, 46.

71. Kimberly J. Lau, "The Social Failure of the Feminist Movement:

A Rhetorical Analysis of Women's Magazines," B.A. honors thesis, University of California, Berkeley, 1990, and Robin Pogrebin, "Adding Sweat and Muscle to a Familiar Formula," *New York Times*, 21 Sept. 1997, sec. 3, p. 1.

72. Pogrebin, sec. 3, p. 1.

73. Pogrebin, section 3, p. 1.

74. Suzanna Markstein, "Less Inner Thigh, More Inner Peace: Our Yoga Workout Will Give You Lean, Sexy Legs and a Shot of Serenity, Too. Om, Sweet, Om!" *Mademoiselle*, June 1999, 79-80.

75. Lauren Purcell, "Spa Fitness," *American Health for Women*, Jan.-Feb. 1998, 56.

76. Rona Berg, "Cerebral Fitness," *Working Woman*, Feb. 1995, 60.

77. Ellen Kunes, "Body Management: No-Sweat Fitness," *Working Woman*, Apr. 1990, 119.

78. Purcell, 56, and Berg, 62.

79. Kunes, 119, and Rebecca Johnson, "Yoga Finds Its Center," *Vogue*, Sept. 1995, 428.

80. Rachel Urquhart, "Mind/Body Exercise." *Vogue*, Feb. 1992, 148, and Berg, 78.

81. Stacey Colino, "Harness the Energy: Eastern Mind-Body Concept Known as Qi," *Women's Sports and Fitness*, Nov.-Dec. 1996, 44.

82. Berg, 78.

83. Urquhart, 144.

84. June Naylor Rodriguez, "Yoga Not Just for Flower Children Anymore," *The Tampa Tribune*, 20 May 1995, 11.

85. Bill Nichols, *Ideology and the Image* (Bloomington: Indiana University Press, 1981).

86. Quoted in Nanci Hellmich, "How Aging Stars Keep Their Svelte Luster," *USA Today*, 3 Jan. 1996, Accent sec., p. 1. See Chapter 3 for the cultural importance of being a size 6 as described by a woman with an eating disorder.

Chapter 5. Risks of Modernity

1. J. J. Clarke, *Oriental Enlightenment: The Encounter Between Asian and Western Thought* (London: Routledge, 1997), 27.

2. See Jürgen Habermas, *The Structural Transformation of the Public Sphere*, trans. Thomas Burger and F. Lawrence (Cambridge: MIT

Press, 1989 [1964]) and Jürgen Habermas, "Further Reflections on the Public Sphere," in *Habermas and the Public Sphere*, ed. Craig Calhoun (Cambridge: MIT Press, 1996 [1992]), 421-461.

3. Ulrich Beck, *Risk Society*, trans. Mark Ritter (London: Sage Publications, 1992), 92.

4. Beck, 100.

5. Kathleen A. Hughes, "In the '90s, Ultimate Status Is Anti-Status," *Wall Street Journal*, 6 Oct. 1996, sec. H, p. 1.

Bibliography

Abrahams, Roger. "Phantoms of Romantic Nationalism in Folkloristics." *Journal of American Folklore* 106 (1993): 3-37.

Alexander, Elizabeth. "'Can You Be BLACK and Look at This?': Reading the Rodney King Video(s)." In *The Black Public Sphere*, edited by the Black Public Sphere Collective. Chicago: University of Chicago Press, 1995, 81-98.

Anderson, Benedict. *Imagined Communities: Reflections on the Origin and Spread of Nationalism*. London: Verso, 1983.

Appadurai, Arjun. "Putting Hierarchy in Its Place." *Cultural Anthropology* 3 (1988): 36-49.

Austin, Regina. "'A Nation of Thieves': Consumption, Commerce, and the Black Public Sphere." In *The Black Public Sphere*, edited by the Black Public Sphere Collective. Chicago: University of Chicago Press, 1995, 229-254.

Baker, Houston Jr. "Critical Memory and the Black Public Sphere." In *The Black Public Sphere*, edited by the Black Public Sphere Collective. Chicago: University of Chicago Press, 1995, 5-38.

Ball, John. *Ananda: Where Yoga Lives*. Bowling Green: Bowling Green University Press, 1982.

Baudrillard, Jean. *The System of Objects*. Translated by James Benedict. New York: Verso, 1996 [1968].

Beck, Ulrich. *Risk Society*. Translated by Mark Ritter. London: Sage Publications, 1992.

Becker, Ingrid. "Coalition Claims Protection from Fragrances under ADA." *Marin Independent Journal*, 27 Jan. 1992, p. 1.

Belasco, Warren J. *Appetite for Change*. New York: Pantheon Books, 1989.

Bendix, Regina. *In Search of Authenticity: The Foundation of Folklore Studies*. Madison: University of Wisconsin Press, 1997.

Berg, Rona. "Cerebral Fitness." *Working Woman*, Feb. 1995, 60-62.

Bhabha, Homi. *The Location of Culture*. London: Routledge, 1994.

Birch, Beryl Bender. *Power Yoga: The Total Strength and Flexibility Workout*. New York: Simon and Schuster, 1995.

Blecher, Michele Bitoun. "Executive Health and Fitness: From Left-of-Center to the Executive Suite: Meditation, Yoga and Other Mind-Body Exercises Find Business Audience." *Crain's Chicago Business*, 20 Jan. 1997, sec. H, p. 1.

Bly, Robert. *Iron John: A Book About Men*. New York: Vintage, 1990.

Bongiorno, Lori. "Beth Pritchard Has Big Plans for Bath & Body Works." *Business Week*, 4 Aug. 1997, 79.

Bordo, Susan. *Unbearable Weight: Feminism, Western Culture, and the Body*. Berkeley: University of California Press, 1993.

Bourdieu, Pierre. *Distinction: A Social Critique of the Judgement of Taste*. Translated by Richard Nice. Cambridge: Harvard University Press, 1984.

Boyd, Todd. "Check Yo Self, Before You Wreck Yo Self: Variations on a Political Theme in Rap Music and Popular Culture." In *The Black Public Sphere*, edited by the Black Public Sphere Collective. Chicago: University of Chicago Press, 1995, 293-316.

Brant, John. "Power Yoga—A New Form of an Ancient Practice Builds Strength and Endurance." *Seattle Times*, 31 Jan. 1996, sec. E, p. 1.

Breslow, Arieh Lev. *Beyond the Closed Door: Chinese Culture and the Creation of T'ai Chi Ch'uan*. Jerusalem: Almond Blossom Press, 1995.

Brown, Denise Whichello. *Teach Yourself Aromatherapy*. Chicago: NTC Publishing Group, 1996.

Calhoun, Craig, ed. *Habermas and the Public Sphere*. Cambridge: MIT Press, 1996 [1992].

Campbell, Bruce F. *Ancient Wisdom Revived: A History of the Theosophical Movement*. Berkeley: University of California Press, 1980.

Campbell, Colin. "The Sociology of Consumption." In *Acknowledging Consumption*, edited by Daniel Miller. London: Routledge, 1991, 96-126.

Canedy, Dana. "Estee Lauder Is Acquiring Maker of Natural Cosmetics." *New York Times*, 20 Nov. 1997, sec. D, p. 4.

Cantwell, Robert. *Ethnomimesis: Folklore and the Representation of Culture*. Chapel Hill: University of North Carolina Press, 1993.

Cavallo, Dominick. *Muscles and Morals: Organized Playgrounds and Urban Reform, 1880-1920*. Philadelphia: University of Pennsylvania Press, 1981.

Christensen, Alice. *The American Yoga Association's New Yoga Challenge: Powerful Workouts for Flexibility, Strength, Energy, and Inner Discovery*. Lincolnwood, Ill.: Contemporary Books, 1997.

Clarke, J.J. *Oriental Enlightenment: The Encounter Between Asian and Western Thought*. London: Routledge, 1997.

Classen, Constance, David Howes, and Anthony Synnott. *Aroma: The Cultural History of Smell*. London: Routledge, 1994.

Colino, Stacey. "Harness the Energy: Eastern Mind-Body Concept Known as Qi." *Women's Sports and Fitness*, Nov.–Dec. 1996, 44-48.

Colwell, Shelley M. "Aromatherapy: Waiting to Inhale." *Soap-Cosmetics-Chemical Specialties*, Dec. 1996, 35-40.

Cooksley,Valerie Gennari. *Aromatherapy: A Lifetime Guide to Healing with Essential Oils*. Englewood Cliffs, N.J.: Prentice-Hall, 1996.

Crompton, Paul H. *The Art of T'ai Chi*. Rockport, Mass.: Element, 1993.

Crystal, David, ed. *The Cambridge Factfinder*. Cambridge: Cambridge University Press, 1993.

Cushman, Anne. "Iyengar Looks Back." *Yoga Journal*, Nov.–Dec. 1997, 84-91 and 156-165.

Damian, Peter and Kate Damian. *Aromatherapy: Scent and Psyche. Using Essential Oils for Physical and Emotional Well-Being*. Rochester, Vt.: Healing Arts Press, 1995

Dawson, Michael C. "A Black Counterpublic? Economic Earthquakes, Racial Agenda(s), and Black Politics." In *The Black Public Sphere*, edited by the Black Public Sphere Collective. Chicago: University of Chicago Press, 1995, 199-228.

Delza, Sophia. *The T'ai Chi Ch'uan Experience: Reflections and Perceptions on Body-Mind Harmony*. Albany: State University of New York Press, 1996.

Dodt, Colleen K. *The Essential Oils Book: Creating Personal Blends for Mind and Body*. Pownal, Vt.: Storey Communications, 1996.

Douglas, Ann. *The Feminization of American Culture*. New York: Knopf, 1977.

Dundes, Alan. "Nationalistic Inferiority Complexes and the Fabrication of Folklore." *Journal of Folklore Research* 22 (1985): 5-18.

Dye, Jane. *First Steps in Aromatherapy*. Essex: C.W. Daniels, 1996.

Ellison, Julie. *Emerson's Romantic Style*. Princeton: Princeton University Press, 1984.

Emerson, Ralph Waldo. *The Collected Works of Ralph Waldo Emerson*, vol. 1. Cambridge: Belknap Press of Harvard University, 1971.

Evans, Mark. *Instant Aromatherapy for Stress Relief*. New York: Lorenz Books, 1996.

Fabian, Johannes. *Time and the Other: How Anthropology Makes Its Object*. New York: Columbia University Press, 1983.

Farr, Joy. "Of Swords, Words and the Necessity of Elders. It's Time for a New Generation of Mentors to Awaken the Spirit of Inspiration in the Young." *The Press Enterprise* (Riverside, Calif.), 9 Oct. 1997, sec. E, p. 1.

Featherstone, Mike. *Consumer Culture and Postmodernism*. London: Sage Publications, 1991.

Feller, Robyn M. *Practical Aromatherapy: Understanding and Using Essential Oils to Heal the Mind and Body*. New York: Berkley Books, 1997.

Feuerstein, Georg. *Textbook of Yoga*. London: Rider, 1975.

———. *The Yoga-Sūtra of Patañjali*. Kent: Wm. Dawson and Sons, 1979.

Fischer-Rizzi, Susanne. *Complete Aromatherapy Handbook: Essential Oils for Radiant Health*. New York: Sterling, 1990.

Fraser, Nancy. "Rethinking the Public Sphere: A Contribution to the Critique of Actually Existing Democracy." In *Habermas and the Public Sphere*, edited by Craig Calhoun. Cambridge, Mass.: MIT Press, 1996 [1992], 109-142.

Frazer, James G. *The Golden Bough*. New York: Oxford University Press, 1994 [1911].

Gebauer, Gunter, and Christoph Wulf. *Mimesis: Culture, Art, Society*. Translated by Don Reneau. Berkeley: University of California Press, 1995 [1992].

Gilroy, Paul. "'After the Love Has Gone': Bio-Politics and Etho-Poetics in the Black Public Sphere." In *The Black Public Sphere*, edited by the Black Public Sphere Collective. Chicago: University of Chicago Press, 1995, 53-80.

Gladwell, Malcolm. "Annals of Style: The Coolhunt." *New Yorker*, 17 March 1997, 77-88.

Golden, Stephanie. "Like Father, Like Son: Looking for a Way to Live a Sane Life in a 'Crazy City,' New Yorkers Are Flocking to Mani and Alan Finger's Ishta Yoga." *Yoga Journal,* Aug. 1994, 36-38, 40.

Goldman, Robert. *Reading Ads Socially.* London: Routledge, 1992.

Green, Harvey. *Fit for America: Health, Fitness, Sport, and American Society*. New York: Pantheon Books, 1986.

Gregory, Steven. "Race, Identity and Political Activism: The Shifting Contours of the African American Public Sphere." In *The Black Public Sphere*, edited by the Black Public Sphere Collective. Chicago: University of Chicago Press, 1995, 151-168.

Grow, Doug. "Smelling Good Can Be Trouble." *Minneapolis-St. Paul Tribune*, 9 Nov. 1994, sec. F, p. 8.

Habermas, Jürgen. "Further Reflections on the Public Sphere." In *Habermas and the Public Sphere*, edited by Craig Calhoun. Cambridge: MIT Press, 1996 [1992]), 421-461.

Hall, Stuart. "The Local and the Global: Globalization and Ethnicity." In *Culture, Globalization and the World-System: Contemporary Conditions for the Representation of Identity*, edited by Anthony D. King. Binghamton: State University of New York Press, 1991, 19-39.

———. "Notes on Deconstructing 'The Popular.'" In *People's History and Socialist History*, edited by Samuel Raphael. London: Routledge and Kegan Paul, 1981, 228-233.

———. "Old and New Identities, Old and New Ethnicities." In *Culture, Globalization and the World-System: Contemporary Conditions for the Representation of Identity*, edited by Anthony D. King. Binghamton: State University of New York Press, 1991, 41-68.

Handler, Richard. *Nationalism and the Politics of Culture in Quebec.* Madison: University of Wisconsin Press, 1988.

Hayes, Alan. *Health Scents*. San Francisco: HarperCollins, 1995.

Heath, Rebecca Piirto. "Beyond the Fringe in the 1990s." *American Demographics*, June 1997, 27-28.

Hellmich, Nanci. "How Aging Stars Keep Their Svelte Luster." *USA Today,* 3 Jan. 1996, Accent sec., p. 1.

Herbstman, Sharon. "Paradise Ain't Perfect: Sivananda Ashram Yoga Retreat." *Women's Sports and Fitness*, March 1997, 32-33.

Herzfeld, Michael. *Ours Once More: Folklore, Ideology, and the Making of Modern Greece.* Austin: University of Texas Press, 1982.

Hodder, Alan D. *Emerson's Rhetoric of Revelation: Nature, the Reader, and the Apocalypse Within*. University Park: Pennsylvania State University Press, 1989.

Hooton, Claire. *T'ai Chi for Beginners: Ten Minutes to Health and Fitness*. New York: Berkley, 1996.

Hopkins, Cathy. *Thorsons Principles of Aromatherapy*. San Francisco: HarperCollins, 1996.

Huang, Alfred. *T'ai Chi: The Definitive Guide to Physical and Emotional Self-Improvement*. Boston: Charles E. Tuttle, 1993.

Hughes, Kathleen A. "In the '90s, Ultimate Status Is Anti-Status." *Wall Street Journal*, 6 Oct. 1996, sec. H, p. 1.

Hymes, Dell. "Folklore's Nature and the Sun's Myth." *Journal of American Folklore* 88 (1975): 345-369.

Jackson, Carl. *The Oriental Religions and American Thought*. Westport, Conn.: Greenwood Press, 1981.

Johnson, Rebecca. "Yoga Finds Its Center." *Vogue*, Sept. 1995, 426-428.

Kaptchuk, Ted J. "Historical Context of the Concept of Vitalism in Complementary and Alternative Medicine." In *Fundamentals of Complementary and Alternative Medicine*, edited by Marc S. Micozzi. New York: Churchill Livingstone, 1996, 35-48.

Keller, Erich. *Aromatherapy Handbook for Beauty, Hair, and Skin Care*. Translated by Christine Grimm. Rochester, Vt.: Healing Arts Press, 1991.

Keville, Kathi. *Pocket Guide to Aromatherapy*. Freedom, Calif.: Crossing Press, 1996.

Keville, Kathi, and Mindy Green. *Aromatherapy: A Complete Guide to the Healing Art*. Freedom: Crossing Press, 1995.

Knutson-Strack, Amy. "CTFA [Cosmetic, Toiletry, and Fragrance Association] Scientific Conference and Annual Trade Show: Adverse Reactions and Claims." *Cosmetics and Toiletries*, Feb. 1997, 35.

Kuhn, Mary Ellen. "Courting Crossover Vegetarian Consumers." *Food Processing*, June 1996, 26-31.

Kunes, Ellen. "Body Management: No-Sweat Fitness." *Working Woman*, Apr. 1990, 119-120.

Kushi, Aveline, and Wendy Esko. *The Quick and Natural Macrobiotic Cookbook*. Chicago: Contemporary Books, 1989.

Kushi, Michio, and Stephen Blauer. *The Macrobiotic Way: The Complete Macrobiotic Diet and Exercise Book*. Garden Park City, N.Y.: Avery, 1985.

Kushi, Michio, and Edward Esko. *Holistic Health Through Macrobiotics*. New York: Japan Publications, 1993.

Lattin, Don. "Just Men Being (New) Men: Poet Robert Bly's Gatherings Are Modern Versions of Initiation Rites." *San Francisco Chronicle*, 15 March 1990, sec. B, p. 3.

Lau, Kimberly J. "The Social Failure of the Feminist Movement: A Rhetorical Analysis of Women's Magazines." B.A. honors thesis, University of California, Berkeley, 1990.

Laurence, Charles. "Wellbeing: You Don't Need Weights and Machines to Work Out. Charles Laurence Watches New Yorkers Being Put Through Their Paces in Central Park." *Daily Telegraph*, 10 Oct. 1997, p. 22.

Lavabre, Marcel. *Aromatherapy Workbook*. Rochester, Vt.: Healing Arts Press, 1997 [1990].

Lawless, Julia. *Aromatherapy and the Mind: An Exploration into the Psychological and Emotional Effects of Essential Oils*. San Francisco: HarperCollins, 1994.

Leaf, Alexander. "A Scientist Visits Some of the World's Oldest People: 'Every Day Is a Gift When You Are Over 100'." *National Geographic*, January 1973, pp. 92-119.

Lears, T. J. Jackson. *No Place of Grace: Antimodernism and the Transformation of American Culture, 1880-1920*. New York: Pantheon Books, 1981.

Liao, Waysun. *T'ai Chi Classics*. Boston: Shambhala, 1990.

Lopez, Alan. *Reality Construction in an Eastern Mystical Cult*. New York: Garland, 1992.

Lortie, Marie-Claude. "Lotus Blossoms: Demystified Yoga Becomes a Growth Industry." *Los Angeles Times*, 19 June 1997, sec. D, p. 1.

Lunt, Peter K., and Sonia M. Livingstone. *Mass Consumption and Personal Identity: Everyday Economic Experience*. Philadelphia: Open University Press, 1992.

Malcolm, Christine. "In Search of Rare Essences for Green-Minded Consumers: Fragrances and Flavors." *Drug and Cosmetic Industry*, May 1994, 24-28.

Market Intelligence Service, Ltd. "Bath & Body Works Aromatherapy Linen Spray—Pure Refreshment." *Market Intelligence Survey, Ltd. Product Alert* 13 (1997): 1.

Markstein, Suzanna. "Less Inner Thigh, More Inner Peace: Our Yoga

Workout Will Give You Lean, Sexy Legs and a Shot of Serenity, Too. Om, Sweet, Om!" *Mademoiselle*, June 1999, 79-80.

McCracken, Grant. *Culture and Consumption: New Approaches to the Symbolic Character of Consumer Goods and Activities*. Bloomington: Indiana University Press, 1988.

McHugh, Fionnuala. "Taking Lauder Back to Nature." *South China Morning Post*, 22 Jan. 1997, Style section, p. 19.

Myer, Charles F. "The Use of Aromatics in Ancient Mesopotamia." Ph.D. diss., University of Pennsylvania, 1975. Ann Arbor: University Microfilms International, 1975. AAC 7612314.

Narayan, Kirin. "Refractions of the Field at Home: American Representations of Hindu Holy Men in the Nineteenth and Twentieth Centuries." *Cultural Anthropology* 8 (1993): 476-509.

Newhouse News Service. "Destroyer or Savior? Impending Yantze Dam Divides Chinese People." *St. Louis Post-Dispatch*, 28 Dec. 1997, sec. A, p. 5.

Nichols, Bill. *Ideology and the Image*. Bloomington: Indiana University Press, 1981.

Ohsawa, George. *Essential Ohsawa: From Food to Health, Happiness to Freedom*. Edited by Carl Ferré. Garden City Park, N.Y.: Avery, 1994.

Pandit, Moti Lal. *Towards Transcendence: A Historico-Analytical Study of Yoga as a Method of Liberation*. New Delhi: Intercultural, 1991.

Park, Roberta J. "Healthy, Moral, and Strong: Educational Views of Exercise and Athletics in Nineteenth-Century America." In *Fitness in American Culture: Images of Health, Sport, and the Body, 1830-1940*, edited by Kathryn Grover. Amherst: University of Massachusetts Press, 1989, 123-168.

Parks, Liz. "Scents for the Soul: Aromatherapy Line Aims at Mass Market." *Drug Store News*, 16 June 1997, 1.

Pirello, Christina. *Cooking the Whole Foods Way: Your Complete, Everyday Guide to Healthy, Delicious Eating with Five Hundred Recipes*. New York: Berkley Publishing Group, 1997.

Pogrebin, Robin. "Adding Sweat and Muscle to a Familiar Formula." *New York Times*, 21 Sept. 1997, sec. 3, p. 1.

PR Newswire. "The Estee Lauder Companies Inc. to Acquire Aveda Corporation, Leading Hair and Beauty Company." *PR Newswire Association, Inc.*, 19 Nov. 1997.

Purcell, Lauren. "Spa Fitness." *American Health for Women*, Jan.–Feb. 1998, 56-57.

Radford, Joan. *The Complete Book of Family Aromatherapy*. London: Foulsham, 1993.

Reinhardt, Susan G. "Yoga Class Is a Fun Class at Gold's." *Asheville Citizen Times*, 28 Nov. 1995, sec. C, p. 5.

Rodriguez, June Naylor. "Yoga Not Just for Flower Children Anymore." *Tampa Tribune*, 20 May 1995, p. 11.

Rosaldo, Renato. "Imperialist Nostalgia." *Representations* 26 (Spring 1989): 107-122.

Rose, Jeanne, and Susan Earle, eds. *The World of Aromatherapy*. Berkeley: North Atlantic Books, 1996.

———. *Herbs and Aromatherapy for the Reproductive System*. Berkeley: Frog, Ltd., 1994.

Rosenberg, Z'ev. "It's Your Metabolism, Not Your Diet." *Macrobiotics Today*, July–Aug. 1994, *http://www.natural-connection.com/resource /default.html*.

Ross-Flanigan, Nancy. "It's Only Natural: Psychologists Studying Humans' Relationship with Environment." *Dallas Morning News*, 18 Dec. 1996, sec. D, p. 8.

Rossi, Barbara, and Glory Schloss. *Everyday Macrobiotic Cookbook*. New York: Universal, 1971.

Rostler, Suzanne. "Anti-Scent Sentiment Catching on in Offices." *Cleveland Plain Dealer*, 16 July 1993, sec. E, p. 1.

Ryan, Mary P. "Gender and Public Access: Women's Politics in Nineteenth-Century America." In *Habermas and the Public Sphere*, edited by Craig Calhoun. Cambridge: MIT Press, 1996 [1992], 259-288.

Ryman, Daniele. *Aromatherapy: The Complete Guide to Plant and Flower Essences for Health and Beauty*. New York: Bantam Books, 1991.

Said, Edward. *Orientalism*. New York: Pantheon Books, 1978.

Schiller, David, and Carol Schiller. *Aromatherapy for Mind and Body*. New York: Sterling, 1996.

Sedlar, Jean. *India in the Mind of Germany: Schelling, Schopenhauer and Their Times*. Washington, D.C.: University Press of America, 1982.

Shields, Rob, ed. *Lifestyle Shopping: The Subject of Consumption*. New York: Routledge, 1992.

Simmel, Georg. *The Philosophy of Money*. Translated by Tom Bottomore and David Frisby. Boston: Routledge and Kegan Paul, 1978 [1906].

Sixel, L. M. "Businesses Try to Limit Fragrances. Move Delights Sensitive Workers." *Houston Chronicle*, 2 Feb., 1995, sec. B, p. 1.

Spencer, Colin. *The Heretic's Feast: A History of Vegetarianism*. London: Fourth Estate, 1993.

Stacey, Michelle. *Consumed: Why Americans Love, Hate, and Fear Food*. New York: Touchstone, 1994.

Stern, Daniel. "Macrobiotic Meals Get 'Ritzy'." *Washington Post*, 27 Aug. 1997, Food sec., p. 1.

Stewart, Susan. *On Longing: Narratives of the Miniature, the Gigantic, the Souvenir, the Collection*. Baltimore: Johns Hopkins University Press, 1984.

Tang, Rose. "No Turning Back Now: For Good or Ill, China's Three Gorges Dam Moves Ahead." *Asiaweek*, 21 Nov. 1997, 42.

Taussig, Michael. *Mimesis and Alterity*. London: Routledge, 1993.

Thomas, Wendell. *Hinduism Invades America*. New York: Beacon Press, 1930.

Tisserand, Maggie. *Aromatherapy for Women: A Practical Guide to Essential Oils for Health and Beauty*. Rochester, Vt.: Healing Arts Press, 1996 [1985].

Tisserand, Robert B. *Aromatherapy: To Heal and Tend the Body*. Wilmot: Lotus Press, 1998.

———. *The Art of Aromatherapy*. Rochester, Vt.: Healing Arts Press, 1985 [1977]).

Turner, Victor. *A Forest of Symbols*. Ithaca: Cornell University Press, 1970.

———. *The Ritual Process*. Ithaca: Cornell University Press, 1977.

Urquhart, Rachel. "Mind/Body Exercise." *Vogue*, Feb. 1992, 139-148.

Walji, Hasnain. *The Healing Power of Aromatherapy: The Enlightened Person's Guide to the Physical, Emotional, and Spiritual Benefits of Essential Oils*. Rocklin, Calif.: Prima, 1996.

Warner, Michael. "The Mass Public and the Mass Subject." In *Habermas and the Public Sphere*, edited by Craig Calhoun. Cambridge: MIT Press, 1996 [1992], 377-401.

Whorton, James C. "Eating to Win: Popular Concepts of Diet, Strength, and Energy in the Early Twentieth Century." In *Fitness in American Culture: Images of Health, Sport, and the Body, 1830-1940*, edited by Kathryn Grover. Amherst: University of Massachusetts Press, 1989, 86-122.

Willis, Susan. *Primer for Daily Life*. New York: Routledge, 1991.

Willson, A. Leslie. *A Mythical Image: The Ideal of India in German Romanticism*. Durham, N.C.: Duke University Press, 1964.

Wilson, William A. *Folklore, Nationalism and Politics in Modern Finland*. Bloomington: Indiana University Press, 1976.

Yogananda. *Autobiography of a Yogi*. Los Angeles: Self-Realization Fellowship, 1993 [1946].

Zaret, David. "Religion, Science, and Printing in the Public Spheres in Seventeenth-Century England." In *Habermas and the Public Sphere*, edited by Craig Calhoun. Cambridge: MIT Press, 1996 [1992], 212-235.

Acknowledgments

Trying to acknowledge fully—and at all adequately—those who have helped me with this project is a more difficult undertaking than the work itself. Yet it is one that I attempt with great pleasure.

First, I would like to thank the English Department and the Women's Studies Program at the University of Utah for inviting me to present an overview of this work in its early stages of development. The enthusiastic, engaging, and challenging discussion that followed my presentation helped me clarify and refine many of my ideas. In particular, I would like to thank Kathryn Stockton and Tomo Hattori for their respective questions about luxury and the political nature of the public sphere of alternative health. Together, the two questions helped me better articulate my concluding arguments.

It is an immense pleasure to thank Regina Bendix for the extraordinarily helpful conversations we had throughout the many stages of this project. The magnitude of Regina's intellect is matched only by the expansiveness of her spirit. She has always been extremely generous with her insights and with her time, and I am lucky to have her as a mentor, a colleague, and a friend. The comments she made in response to this work were not only challenging and critical but also fundamental to my own thinking. Regina's ideas resonate throughout this book in ways that are difficult to acknowledge with references and citations.

I am also happy to thank Janet Theophano, Roger Abrahams, Meg Brady, and Patricia Smith, all great intellects who have gone way beyond the call of duty in reading and responding to my work both as it was emerging and as it needed reshaping and rethinking. As always, Janet guided me toward a better understanding of the political implications of my material, and Roger provided me with the essential historical contexts for my arguments. Meg pushed in exactly the right places, gently forcing me to make explicit the logic that made sense only in my head, and Patricia encouraged me to free myself from what I imagined to be the restraints of academic writing, thus making for much more enjoyable, jargon-free prose.

I am tremendously grateful to Tim Warner for creating the beautiful and witty "Capitalist Buddha" that sits on the book's cover. I would also like to thank everyone who clipped news articles about everything from aromatherapy soaps to yoga among the rich and famous. In this regard, I am especially indebted to Dan Kinnard for the steady supply of yoga catalogs and New Age magazines and newspapers. I am also happy to thank my mother, Eloise Lau, and my grandmother, Joyce Tashima, for funding the "rewards" I used as incentives for completing the various chapters on time. Without them, I wouldn't have been able to enjoy all those massages, facials, and indulgent vacations to Hawaii and the Cayman Islands! My mother is also a professional librarian, and I cannot thank her enough for her research prowess and her willingness to help me out on some especially tight deadlines. I owe a huge debt of gratitude to Sheila Wills, computer goddess, who spent countless hours retrieving my manuscript every time it ended up in that unknown place where files go when computers crash. Without her, there would be no book, and no amount of chocolate or flowers or Mexican food can even begin to repay my debt to her. I also owe many thanks to Joy Sather-Wagstaff for her detailed and thorough work on the index.

I am very fortunate to have an amazing community of smart, generous, spirited friends whose willingness to teach and to think, to talk, travel, play, and go mountain-biking in red-rock country has ensured that these past two years of writing have not been dull or injury-free. More than any New Age discourses, they remind me why balance matters in life and in biking.

Index